The Future of Live

The Future of Live

Karin van Es

polity

First published in 2017 by Polity Press

Polity Press
65 Bridge Street
Cambridge CB2 1UR, UK

Polity Press
350 Main Street
Malden, MA 02148, USA

ISBN-13: 978-1-5095-0263-9
ISBN-13: 978-1-5095-0264-6(pb)

A catalogue record for this book is available from the British Library.

Typeset in 10.5 on 12 pt Sabon
by Toppan Best-set Premedia Limited
Printed and bound in Great Britain by Clays Ltd, St. Ives PLC

The publisher has used its best endeavours to ensure that the URLs for external websites referred to in this book are correct and active at the time of going to press. However, the publisher has no responsibility for the websites and can make no guarantee that a site will remain live or that the content is or will remain appropriate.

Every effort has been made to trace all copyright holders, but if any have been inadvertently overlooked the publisher will be pleased to include any necessary credits in any subsequent reprint or edition.

For further information on Polity, visit our website: politybooks.com

Contents

Preface   *vi*

Acknowledgments   *viii*

1 Introduction   1

2 Constellations of Liveness   18

3 Liveness and Institutionalization   35

4 "Live" as an Evaluative Category   64

5 Social TV and the Multiplicity of the Live   83

6 Social Media's New Relation to the Live   123

Conclusions   152

Notes   *163*

Resources   *173*

References   *176*

Index   *190*

Preface

Liveness has been, and still is, a persistent and much-debated concept in media studies. The emergence of social media, following the dot-com bubble bust of the early 2000s, has brought new forms of liveness into effect. These challenge common assumptions about and perspectives on liveness, and provoke a revisiting of the concept. This book develops a comprehensive understanding of what liveness is and seeks to clarify the stakes surrounding the category of the "live."

So far, considerations of liveness have been partial: they tend to be limited in outlook to the notion's relevance to the particular cases under scrutiny. As such, they promote either an ontological, phenomenological, or rhetorical perspective on the live. Each of these perspectives highlights some but obscures other dimensions of the notion. Reinterpreting liveness for the social media era, this book develops a method by which to combine those perspectives, charting liveness in terms of "constellations." By analyzing the live as it manifests itself in four cases (Livestream, e-Jamming, *The Voice*, and Facebook), it explores the operation of the category of liveness and pinpoints the conditions under which it comes into being. The analyses it provides also facilitate a comparison of the mechanisms of control of broadcast media and social media, and a broader reflection on how these media relate to each other.

Specifically, the book should be of interest to upper-level students and researchers in media studies. It touches upon topics debated by radio, theater, film, television, and new media scholars. For television and new media researchers it is of particular interest, as it raises critical questions about today's social media and how we should envision their relation to broadcast media.

Acknowledgments

This book is the product of a series of encounters and exchanges that took place over the course of several years. Above all, I must thank Eggo Müller and Sonja de Leeuw, not only for the job opportunity that allowed me to obtain my Ph.D., but also for their continued support throughout the research period. I am particularly grateful to Judith Keilbach for sparking my interest in the topic of liveness, and for being a great sparring partner ever since.

I am furthermore greatly indebted to Nick Couldry, who has inspired my thinking on media, and was so generous to meet and discuss with me the ideas for this book. But I also owe thanks to Nanna Verhoeff, William Uricchio, Frank Kessler, José van Dijck, Joost Raessens, and three anonymous reviewers for engaging with my work and raising pertinent questions that have vastly helped sharpen my arguments. My gratitude goes as well to Jim Gibbons, Ronny Temme, and Claudy op den Kamp for their interventions and contributions in the final phase. At Polity, I thank Andrea Drugan and Elen Griffiths for guiding me through the publication process.

Above all, I want to thank my family and friends for their continued encouragement and much-needed sense of relativism. And finally, much affection to Eef, for her critical comments, as well as her love and support every step of the way.

Amsterdam, March 2016

1
Introduction

It's early January 2016, and, over coffee, my neighbor Ronny tells me that several times a year she takes the ferry to the cinema across the IJ lake in Amsterdam to watch broadcasts of operas and ballets staged at London's Royal Opera House in Covent Garden. These performances are simulcast live to 15,000 cinemas in more than thirty-five countries. Ronny speaks enthusiastically of these occasions. She revels in the camerawork and enjoys the comfort of the cinema. During intermissions, she explains, tweets from viewers are displayed on screen, making visible, as it were, other viewers watching in cinemas across the globe. She has a friend in England who also attends these screenings, and afterward they evaluate the performances over the phone.

Ronny's account draws attention to the continuing reliance on the live in our present-day media landscape and raises several important considerations about it. These screenings, for instance, underscore how live broadcasts—contrary to the idea that liveness provides a natural and direct connection to a given occasion—are heavily produced (Caldwell 2000; Scannell 2001). To avoid transmitting "boring" footage of the operas and ballets taken from a single stationary camera, the broadcasts actively switch between cameras, offering multiple points of view. In overall effect, cinemagoers here are offered an experience unlike that of anyone actually present at the performances. This, of course, has been the case for "live" televised sports for at least a half-century. But these live-streamed events also illustrate that the live is no longer a property of radio or television alone; the "live" media landscape is now multifarious. Not only do services like Twitter make their own claims to be live, but they also intersect with traditional forms of liveness. In the above example, Twitter interacts with the streaming video shown in theaters worldwide, as audience members are actively invited to comment on the performance.

That the descriptor "live" has been used in relation to multiple media forms has magnified the confusion about what it means for a medium to be live. People tend to have a general notion of the term's meaning. But when ideas about the "live" are put to critical scrutiny, the concept proves to be more complex than one might think. Consider these opera and ballet simulcasts: when they're being promoted as live, what is actually being promised? Why does it matter that they are "live"? What do viewers expect from them?

Philip Auslander (2008) has traced the origins of the term "live" to 1934, when broadcast media confused the opposition between live and recorded performances, creating a "crisis." He explains the crisis in terms of how "radio [unlike the gramophone] does not allow you to see the sources of the sounds you are hearing; therefore, you can never be sure if they are live or recorded" (Auslander 2008, 59). "Live" was introduced as a term so that the distinction could be made in these cases as well (ibid., 60). That radio was a "live" medium to begin with had been a matter of strategic choice. As Robert Vianello explains,

> The emergence of "live" radio was not only a mechanism to install centralized production/distribution of "programs" over local production/distribution, it is also the mechanism that installed the broadcast agent as the voice of concentrated capital, centralized production and mass consumption. (Vianello 1985, 28)

The same was true with the development of television. In fact, in the thirties, there were several experiments in Europe with television prototypes that were dependent on recorded images. However, television's ability to electronically transmit live images was preferred in the United States, and that ability had a substantial impact on the formation of the networks and dominance of the television industry. Drawing upon their technical and structural experiences in radio, network broadcasters conceived electronic television as a means of transmitting images from point to point. (Friedman 2002, 3)

The post–World War II years marked the beginning of commercial television broadcasting in the United States. In terms of programming, from the late forties to the sixties, live anthology dramas (e.g., *The Philco Television Playhouse* [NBC, 1948–1955]) proliferated. These were initially Broadway plays and adaptations of classic theater that made the new medium quite attractive to a mass audience. They became the defining characteristic of what is now known as the Golden Age of Television. Television networks used their live programming to differentiate themselves aesthetically from film (Caldwell 1995, 38) and to deter competition in the distribution space. Transcribed programming, the alternative, would have made independent syndication possible and paved the way for non-network distribution, as indeed later happened (Vianello 1985, 27–31). In short, the electronic transmission of live images was "not television's technological destiny, but rather an identifying characteristic that could be used when strategically necessary, convenient, or profitable" (Friedman 2002, 4).

By the fifties and sixties the networks had secured their position and programming was increasingly filmed or taped (Bourdon 2000, 183). This approach gained prominence because it was more profitable for the industry. Regularly scheduled live programming eventually became limited to newscasts, presidential debates, and sports (Friedman 2002, 4), and the occasional outlier such as NBC's long-running *Saturday Night Live* comedy series. Subsequently, the eighties to the 2000s brought the VCR, remote control, and analog cable, providing audiences with more control over when and how they watched television. During this period occasional references were made to the Golden Age through special live programming (e.g., the live season premiere of NBC's *ER* in 1997). According to Elana Levine, these instances can be seen as "struggles over distinction and cultural worth that have long been part of television history, but that take on new dimensions in an altered media environment" (2008, 395). The competition for viewer eyeballs became fiercer in the "post-network era," when the digital video recorder (DVR) and video on demand (VOD) gave viewers more choice over when, where, and how to watch television (Lotz 2014, 8). This period witnessed the popularity of reality-singing competitions, beginning in the 2000s, with shows like *American Idol* (Fox, 2002–2016) and extending to the present with shows like *The Voice* (NBC, 2011–). These programs enabled viewers to participate in live episodes through other "live" media. Despite the changing place of live programming in broadcast television, it retains an important function—one that is explored in depth in this book. Similar to the live experiments discussed by Levine, nowadays live television is used to compete with new viewing platforms and business models such as those represented by Netflix, Amazon Prime, and Hulu. Both event TV (e.g., important sporting events and awards shows) and social TV (i.e., the combination of social media and television) can be understood as popular industry strategies to draw audiences back to watching television live. Promising sociable experiences that depend on watching programming when it first airs, these strategies encourage live viewing—a form of viewership that can be monetized through Nielsen ratings.

Like the account of my neighbor watching her simulcasts, this brief historical reflection on the live in relation to American television highlights the concept's complexity. It problematizes the idea that liveness is simply a property of a particular technology because, as I have noted, it's part of a business strategy as well. We see, moreover, that the live can have multiple reference points; it operates at the level not only of transmission (live broadcast) but also of content (live programming). Yet the issue of the live gets even thornier. Consider the conclusion of Nick Couldry's *Media Rituals: A Critical Approach* (2003), where the author deliberated whether, due to the pervasive influence of the internet and networked technologies, the category live would someday become "less necessary, even redundant" (138). I address at length how he came to speculate about this sort of future scenario in chapter 2. For now, though, it is important to realize that over a decade after Couldry gave voice to this possibility, the live is still being claimed in several media formats, and even seems to be claimed *more* actively than before. Why is this? Here in this book I develop the argument that liveness can be understood as a construction, a product of the interaction among institutions, technologies, and users/ viewers. By analyzing several instances of the live, I hope to contribute to a more comprehensive understanding of this phenomenon and to offer insights into the likelihood of its future survival.

Liveness as a Concept in Media Studies

Although liveness was at first a professional notion, it has been an academic concept central to television studies since the fifties and sixties (Bourdon 2000, 183), even if over time far fewer television programs were broadcast "live." John T. Caldwell (1995) has criticized the concept's centrality in television studies and the discipline's "theoretical obsession" (27) with live TV. Yet despite this critique, the concept has persisted and been picked up in academic writing on "new media" (McPherson 2002; Couldry 2004; Michele White 2006; Ytreberg 2009; Auslander 2012). As I explore in the following pages, liveness in media studies—the perspectives on it and the scholarly assumptions behind it—fail to capture the complexity and multiplicity of the live.

In media studies to date, the concept of the live/liveness has been considered from three main perspectives: as ontology, as phenomenology (located in the audience), and as rhetoric. The distinctions that would differentiate the three perspectives are rather artificial, and thus some accounts fit with more than one perspective. However, by considering, through selected examples, the merits and shortcomings of those three main strands, I wish to lay the foundation for a discussion, at a later stage, of the alternative I propose: one that combines elements of all three perspectives, and in so doing outlines a conception understood as *constellations of liveness*. Liveness, I propose, is best understood as a construction informed by technologies, institutions, and users.

Ontology

In relation to television, it is possible to distinguish two types of ontological claims with regard to liveness, centered, respectively, on the technology of the scanning beam and the possibility for simultaneity among television's production, distribution, and reception. I consider these two forms of reasoning first, then home in on liveness that is seen as the ontology of "new media."

The first type of argument is exemplified by the work of Herbert Zettl (1978), who claimed that television's technological basis is precisely what makes it a "live" process. He writes:

> While in film each frame is actually a static image, the television image is continually moving, very much in the manner of the Bergsonian durée. The scanning beam is constantly trying to complete an always incomplete image. Even if the image on the screen seems at rest, it is structurally in motion. (Zettl 1978, 5)

Stephen Heath and Gillian Skirrow (1977) have discussed liveness as a mode of the televisual in similar terms. They claim:

> In one sense, the television image itself is effectively 'live,' very different in this to that of film. Where the latter depends on the immobility of the frame, the former, electronic and not photographic, is an image in perpetual motion, the movement of a continually scanning beam; whatever the status of the material transmitted, the image as series of electric impulses is necessarily 'as it happens.' Hence the possibility of *performing* the television image—electronic, it can be modified, altered, transformed in the moment of its transmission, is a production in the present. (Heath and Skirrow 1977, 53) ·

Television's difference from film, then, is technological: TV is electronic rather than photographic. Unlike Zettl, however, Heath and Skirrow also see liveness as an ideology of the television apparatus, in that it is rooted not only in the medium's electronic nature but in the dimensions of the image, which offers "a permanently *alive* view on the world" (Heath and Skirrow 1977, 54).

The second type of argument that posits television as being ontologically live is based on the medium's capacity to provide simultaneity between the time of production and that of transmission and viewing. As Auslander points out, right from its inception, the essence of the televisual was understood

> as an ontology of liveness more akin to the ontology of theater than to that of film. Television's essence was seen in its ability to transmit events as they occur, not in a filmic capacity to record events for later viewing. Originally, of course, all television broadcasts were live transmissions. (2008, 12)

In some approaches, liveness continues to be seen as an immanent feature of the operation of television. Though television is in fact a patchwork of different media and temporalities (Feuer 1983), liveness is always available as an option due to its electronic features (Marriott 2007; Mumford 1994). But this argument is problematic because it falls prey to a "metonymic fallacy" (Mimi White 2004): liveness is taken as *the* defining characteristic of television simply because television *can* be live.

Along similar lines of reasoning, an argument has been made that is centered on the *organization of transmission*—a view that has gained prominence since the decline of live programming on television. It is found, for example, in the writings of Joshua Meyrowitz. Discussing radio, he argues:

> There is a big difference between listening to a cassette tape while driving in a car and listening to a radio station, in that the cassette player cuts you off from the outside world, while the radio station ties you into it. Even with a local radio station, you are 'in range' of any news about national and world events. (Meyrowitz 1986, 90)

And so, even when a broadcast has been recorded, its transmission is "live," in that programming can be interrupted at any given moment. This is how liveness is now commonly understood (Couldry 2004; Ellis 2000).

The argument that liveness is television's ontological essence has been joined by more recent claims that liveness is the ontological essence of new media. Margaret Morse (1998), for instance, considering interactivity, has written:

> Feedback in the broadest sense...is a capacity of a machine to signal or seem to respond to input instantaneously. A machine that thus 'interacts' with the user even at this minimal level can produce a feeling of 'liveness' and a sense of the machine's agency and—because it exchanges symbols—even of a subjective encounter with a persona. (18)

This is a clear case where technology is seen to cause liveness. Philip Auslander initially subscribed to this position in the second edition of his *Liveness: Performance in a Mediatized Culture* (2008), where he aimed to situate live performance in our mediatized culture, providing a historical overview of the concept. There he claimed that the definition of liveness is rearticulated when a new technology is introduced. Discussing "digital liveness" in relation to interactivity, Auslander suggested that the feedback of real-time interaction is what monocausally establishes liveness.

The notion that liveness is connected to a medium's capacity for instantaneity seems convincing, but due to the ambiguity permitted over how "simultaneous" transmission and reception needs to be (Mimi White 2004), it is flawed. Consider, for instance, how there may sometimes be a slight temporal delay perceptible between different realizations of the same broadcast (e.g., your neighbors are cheering seconds before you see the goal scored on TV). All these media, indeed, are equally understood to provide "live" broadcasts. The accepted ambiguity over what is understood as "live" implies that liveness isn't simply a property of a particular form of technology. Accounts that conceive of liveness as the ontological basis of a particular medium tend to overlook the social dimension of liveness.

That liveness is a social construction cannot be ignored when one considers the implications of the controversy over Janet Jackson's "wardrobe malfunction" during the Super Bowl XXXVIII halftime show in 2004, broadcast live on the CBS television network in the United States and elsewhere around the world. During the show, one of Jackson's nipples was revealed, sparking public debate about indecency on network broadcasting. The incident resulted in the passing of the Broadcast Decency Enforcement Act by the U.S. Congress, signed by President George W. Bush into law in 2005. This act enabled the Federal Communications Commission (FCC), the U.S. government agency responsible for telecommunications regulation, to levy high penalties to broadcasters of profane and/or indecent material between the hours of 6 AM and 10 PM on network television.[1] A breach of the act can result in a $325,000 fine per incident, with a maximum of $3 million per day. The networks have generally responded to these stricter regulations by building short delays into their live broadcasting, allowing for offensive material to be preempted. ABC, for example, implemented a five-second broadcast delay for all live entertainment in 2004, even before the act became law.[2] Yet even after the introduction of transmission delays, these broadcasts continued to be promoted as "live," and that's what they continue to be called in popular discourse.

The perspective that considers liveness as ontology is problematic, because liveness cannot be reduced to a technological fact alone. In making this claim, I do not deny that electronic media share a capacity for instantaneity, but I want to insist that there is more to liveness than that. I develop this argument further in chapter 4, where I compare and contrast liveness to real time in the context of the music-collaboration platform eJamming. For now, it is sufficient to understand that media platforms considered "live" vary in terms of which elements are in fact simultaneous (production/transmission/reception, production/transmission or transmission/reception), and even allow for flexibility when it comes to how simultaneous these elements need to be.

Phenomenology

There are also accounts of liveness that view it as primarily an experience of the viewer or user (Auslander 2008; Dixon 2007; Marriott 2007; Scannell 2014). In 2008, Auslander argued that the emerging definition of liveness (associated with digital technologies) was increasingly built around the audience's affective experience. Initially, however, he saw this as a direct outcome of technological properties. Later, he revisited this claim (Auslander 2012), stating that he regretted the implications of his original formulation. By claiming that the affective responses elicited by media can be explained in terms of their ontological distinctions, he stated, one commits the fallacy of technological determinism. Even so, Auslander thought he was onto something, and his 2012 work continues to view audience experience as the key to understanding liveness.

To solve the problem of technological determinism, while continuing to associate liveness with affective response, he offers the following alternative:

> The benefit of a phenomenological perspective is that it enables us to understand that digital liveness is neither caused by intrinsic properties of virtual entities nor simply constructed by their audiences. Rather, digital liveness emerges as a specific relation between self and other, a particular way of 'being involved with something.' The experience of liveness results from our conscious act of grasping virtual entities as live in response to the claims they make on us. (Auslander 2012, 10)

The updated definition avoids the pitfall of liveness being reduced to a property or effect of a technology. His revision addresses liveness as a construction, effecting the relation between the technology and its user.

Although I applaud Auslander for making this conceptual move, his recent work continues to raise some issues. When Auslander discusses the historical development of the live in his 2012 book, he links types of liveness to particular cultural forms, suggesting a one-sided relationship between liveness and medium and implying that each new medium provides a complete break with other forms of liveness. Instead, it is arguable that media borrow from and refashion earlier conceptions of liveness through a series of "remediations" (Bolter and Grusin 2000). Moreover, Auslander's term "digital liveness" conceals the fact that diverse manifestations of liveness are possible within such a cluster (e.g., live-tweeting and live-blogging might offer two distinct constructions of liveness).

The term not only overemphasizes the role of technology in constructing liveness, but also suggests that digital technologies necessarily share a single definition of "live." Finally, Auslander is unclear about what "the claims [technologies] make on us" (as the above quote puts it) might mean, and about the role such claims play with regard to the experience of liveness.

The work of Paddy Scannell (2001; 2014) offers another account, and it is one worth considering here since it shares insights relevant to the take on the live that I develop in this book. For Scannell, liveness is about lived experience and about being alive. In his work, he studies the "care structures" of radio and broadcast television, looking at "the management and production by broadcasting of speech-act-events as to be experienced live by listeners and viewers situated in their own time and place" (Scannell 2014, 103). Ultimately, he proposes that liveness is a construction, which producers work at to offer genuine experiences that viewers feel they are witnesses of. These experiences are made available to everyone in the same way in real time, making them a "topical resource for subsequent talk" (Scannell 2001, 409). Think here of the example of my friend Ronny discussing the performances at Covent Garden with her friend in England after their visits to their respective cinemas. Because they watched the simulcast "together," as it unfolded, they are entitled to speak about the experience. However, while I too see liveness as a construction (albeit in a somewhat different manner), what I find problematic here is Scannell's avoidance of critical media theory. His phenomenological approach to the study of media focuses on what radio and television *mean* to audiences, thus downplaying the ideological functions of media.

Rhetoric

Finally, numerous academics have discussed liveness as rhetoric. The accounts that I align with this perspective see the "live" construction as part of a producer's strategy. I begin by highlighting the accounts of certain authors who argue that liveness is used as a marker of distinction. I then identify those who specifically tackle the ideological dimensions of liveness as rhetoric, expanding briefly on Jane Feuer's influential claims on the topic. William Boddy underscores the social shaping of technology when he claims:

> Every electronic media product launch or network debut carries with it an implicit fantasy scenario of its domestic consumption, a polemical ontology of its medium, and an ideological rationale for its social function. (2003)

Several media technologies have been promoted as "live," including radio, the telephone, television, and, now, online platforms. With liveness "as rhetoric," I refer to accounts like Boddy's, which analyzes the commercial discourses of "self-serving fantasies of the medium's nature" (2003, 191). For example, competing against pay-television services in the 1950s, the three major American networks of the time strategically boasted of television's live status as a nation-builder and heralded its aesthetic superiority. Because influential marketing techniques are always redefining media, conventional notions about a medium are continually shifting.

In a similar vein, Michele White (2006) finds that television and internet producers invoke liveness to suggest that their content is unmediated. She compares the construction of liveness in the two media, disclosing the politics behind the rendering of interfaces as (a)live. She argues that, politically speaking, this rendering makes users overlook the mediated aspects of these platforms.

Whereas Boddy and White both examine how liveness has been rhetorically used to hierarchize media, Elana Levine (2008) shows how liveness is used to create a hierarchy among television programs. She analyzes the creation of media hierarchies by various discursive attempts that make distinctions between types of programs: for instance in American television's Golden Age, when live anthology drama was differentiated from other programming that was equally live (e.g., daytime shows and soap operas). She also cites the discourses around live experiments with scripted drama and comedy television shows since the 1990s. Rhetorically, Levine argues, these experiments drew on the concept of liveness to position themselves as being "not television."

Other authors, more specifically, have examined the ideological dimensions of liveness as a programming strategy on the level of the text, in relation to television (Vianello 1985; Caldwell 1995; Ellis 2000; Mimi White 2004), the internet (McPherson 2002), and multiplatform formats (Ytreberg 2009). The most influential theorist here is certainly Feuer, who, in her seminal essay "The Concept of Live Television: Ontology as Ideology" (1983), rejected the then-prevailing conviction that liveness is the essence of the television medium. Her account was thus directly opposed to those that positioned liveness as part of the ontology of television. According to Feuer, technological innovations such as computerized graphics and instant replay undermined the basic meaning of "live," located in the simultaneity of event, transmission, and reception. Rather than actually being ontologically live, Feuer argues, television uses its perceived ontology as ideology. To do so, "flow and unity [in television programming] are emphasized giving a sense of immediacy and wholeness" (Feuer 1983, 16). With specific regard to television's mode of address, Feuer has analyzed how in the show *Good Morning America*, liveness helps to overcome fragmentation, allowing for the illusion of directness and presentness. In the essay's concluding remarks, she writes that she is somewhat uncertain about how the program's ideology is reproduced in its audience, and how there might be oppositional readings of the program. Indeed, what her account specifically overlooks— a limitation that Nick Couldry (2003; 2004) aptly pinpoints— is the connection to the larger sociological question of how people participate in this construction.

The benefit of the liveness-as-rhetoric perspective lies in its ability to explain certain things about liveness that the other accounts cannot, because it posits liveness as a construction. This perspective can, for example, account for the fact that liveness is characteristic of a variety of media, as well as for the ambiguity in terms of how simultaneous transmission and reception need to be, and for the concept's persistence over time (Couldry 2004). My problem, however, is that these accounts overemphasize the role of institutions in the construction of liveness. As a result, they overlook the roles that technologies and users play in shaping the live.

Aims of the Book

What the overview of the three different perspectives on liveness clarifies is that while all provide relevant reflections on certain domains of liveness (e.g., technology, users, institutions), none can aptly capture the complexity of live media on its own. Claiming here in this book that liveness is a construction shaped by institutions, technologies, and users, I propose a way to analyze these constructions as particular *constellations of liveness*. I examine how liveness is constructed in a selection of four case studies, in order to accomplish two main goals: to explore the operation and significance of liveness, and to extend and deepen our understanding of the new media ecosystem in what I call the "social media era."[3] This latter aim is possible because in certain cases, I uncover *tensions surrounding the live*: conflicts that emerge in the construction among technologies, users, and institutions with regard to the meaning and promise of the "live." These conflicts make the constructedness of the live visible and help to reveal how media content is managed—on the level of production, distribution, and consumption—in both broadcast media and social media, through what I call *mechanisms of control*.

More specifically, I examine the constellation of liveness in Livestream, eJamming, *The Voice*, and Facebook. I have chosen these examples because these platforms or subsets thereof have explicitly been indexed as "live," and because, taken together, they display considerable diversity, as each platform has a rather different sociotechnical and economic configuration. These four cases help me consider liveness in its plurality, and allow for reflection on the interesting dynamic between broadcast media and social media in our present moment. By examining *The Voice*, I can reflect on social TV and broadcast media more generally, whereas my analysis of Facebook enables a consideration of social media and their feeds. The case studies have been selected with these goals in mind. They also share certain common ground in that they are all American commercial services or products.

Structure of the Book

Having established the need for a more comprehensive understanding of liveness, in chapter 2 I hypothesize on why the live continues to be relevant and expound my proposal to analyze constellations of liveness. The first issue can be explained by addressing how Couldry (2000; 2003; 2004; 2012) has developed liveness as a "media ritual" category, which helps me position liveness as a *construction* involved in naturalizing media power—the concentration of symbolic resources in the principal mass-media entities. Building on this analysis, I argue that the social media era introduces a wide range of forms of liveness and reflect on its participatory culture, wherein new relations are being forged between media institutions and users around content. In relation to the second issue, I expand on my proposed method for analyzing the live, which includes a discussion of the three domains of liveness that inform the constellation: the metatext, the space of participation, and user responses. These domains reflect the formative influence of institutions, technologies, and users on the live.

To ascertain and unravel the relation of the live to institutionalization, chapter 3 investigates the two constellations of liveness that emerged over time for the live-streaming platform Livestream. Livestream is a particularly worthy case in that it provocatively claims to have redefined liveness in transforming itself from a platform for user-generated content to a destination for professional content. Considering this shift and the two distinct constellations involved helps me to parse a *paradox of liveness*: a tension between the constructedness of liveness and the idea of direct and "natural" access to the events relayed. In the chapter, I explore how the Mogulus/Livestream platform first borrowed heavily from the practices of traditional television in its platform design and promoted the purported ability of users to become media moguls themselves. Over time, the company behind the platform acquired a clearer picture of how it was being used and what type of content was most successful at drawing an audience. Learning from this beta testing period, it shifted its focus from democratizing broadcast television to becoming a destination platform for live-event television. Thus the New Livestream platform was introduced, which provocatively claimed to have redefined the "live" in live-streaming. At this point, an alternative constellation of liveness was born. In this chapter, the paradox of liveness is explored through reflections on the need for Livestream to revamp and professionalize the platform.

Chapter 4, which examines the online music-collaboration platform eJamming, exposes the constructedness of the live. In failing to deliver on user expectations of the live, the case furthermore illuminates how liveness operates as an evaluative category. The success—or failure—of eJamming relied in part on its ability to provide simultaneity between the production, distribution, and reception of audio. Therefore, the notion of "real time" becomes particularly important to this constellation. Here I consider how the concepts "live" and "real time," all too often used interchangeably, overlap but also diverge from each other.

Having explored the relation of liveness to institutionalization in chapter 3, and deconstructed the constructedness of liveness in chapter 4, the book then shifts its attention. Having first introduced an approach to liveness, I now move on to using liveness as a tool for comparing broadcast media with social media. I do so by considering the tensions surrounding the live that surface in the case studies. Charting the constellations of liveness in *The Voice* (chapter 5) and Facebook (chapter 6) allows for a comparison between the mechanisms of control that inform these representatives of two different communication models (broadcast media and social media). The assessments offered here help grasp the lines of change and continuity in the production and distribution of media.

Chapter 5 explores the multiplicity of the live through the lens of social TV. The social TV phenomenon is commonly understood as a strategy broadcasters use to return audiences to watching television live; they do so by complementing live broadcasts with the real time of social media. In this chapter, I analyze the live shows of the popular reality-singing competition *The Voice*. *The Voice* offers an interesting layering of liveness constructions within the live shows' constellation, but also in the overlapping spaces of television and social media. By discussing these constructions, I can point to several conditions under which liveness comes to be. This case, furthermore, allows for a consideration of the intensifying relationship between television and social media platforms (e.g., Twitter and Facebook). Here we see emerging two tensions surrounding the live, which I connect to academic discussions on, respectively, the rhythms and temporalities of broadcast media (more specifically, series dumping and data-driven decision-making) and audience participation.

Chapter 6 examines how users these days have established a "new" relation to liveness, in that they can upload and circulate content on social media themselves. As a result, they are no longer only the recipients of live media content, as had been the case in the broadcast era, but are also its producers. In particular, the chapter explores the social networking site Facebook. Here, I analyze Facebook's News Feed feature and its Live Feed subsidiary, which have seen various iterations over the years. The construction of liveness is seen here to revolve primarily around the intensity of (algorithmic) selection made for the user. Again, a tension surrounding the live emerges, focused this time on the fact that users now enjoy a producer relation to liveness. The liveness of the feed promises direct access to the interactions among the platform's users. This tension, one that connects to debates on user privacy, leads me to a series of interconnected reflections and facilitates a comparison between broadcast media and social media.

Concluding the analyses of the different constellations, chapter 7 locates parallels between the manifestations of the live that I have tackled in the book. Here, I detect patterns across the cases that help us understand when and how a platform, or one of its features, is conceived of as "live" in our present-day culture. Together, these reveal when liveness comes into being and how it operates. After a brief reconsideration of the observations made in previous chapters, I discuss how my approach to the live enhances our understanding of contemporary media—and why the concept is likely to persist.

2
Constellations of Liveness

As briefly touched on in the introduction, Nick Couldry, in the final chapter of *Media Rituals: A Critical Approach* (2003), speculates whether the internet and digital technologies make categories such as the live redundant. This thought is prompted by the observation that the new opportunities for production and consumption offered by these technologies might weaken the media's power: the concentration, that is, of symbolic power in the central broadcast media, which allows the media to construct social reality. According to Couldry, liveness is a "media ritual category" that helps to legitimize and maintain the uneven distribution of symbolic power. Over a decade later, we can say that while the internet has helped to change the relation between media institutions and users, it has not fragmented symbolic power but has instead given rise to new concentrations of power (namely in social media).

Couldry's analysis notwithstanding, it is not surprising that liveness has not only remained relevant but has found new forms. Yet as explained in the previous chapter, prevailing academic assumptions and perspectives fail to capture new forms of the live. In this chapter, I develop an approach to liveness that acknowledges that institutions, technologies, and users all play a part in constructing it. I respond to approaches to the live that treat it—reductively—as either a property of technology, an affective experience, or a manifestation of industry rhetoric. The chapter introduces a methodological tool for analyzing articulations of the live and, furthermore, provides a theoretical framework for understanding the live in relation to media power (and, also, user participation).

Media Power and the "Live"

Couldry's work on liveness resulted from his attempt to answer the question of why people place such value on media output. He argues that the media

> provide an essential flow of information and meanings, that enable the generation of new discursive resources at a societal level, both through factual information and through media fictions, such as soaps, which may focus important social debates. (2000, 51)

This is the "symbolic power of the media," and it concerns how "media are involved in our fantasies, our self-images, and our descriptions of reality" (Couldry 2000, 21). To provide evidence of media power, Couldry analyzed how people act and talk when encountering sites of media production (e.g., film locations, the sets of TV shows, and the like). Here he noticed that people adhere to formal boundaries between everyday space and media space, and between what is "in" the media (and therefore of greater significance) and what is "outside."

In his conceptualization of symbolic power, Couldry is specifically critical of what he calls the "weak concept" developed by John B. Thompson (1995). For Thompson, symbolic power is simply the ability

> to intervene in the course of events, to influence the actions of others and indeed to create events, by means of the production and transmission of symbolic forms. (1995, 17)

Couldry favors Bourdieu's "strong concept" of symbolic power, because it acknowledges that some concentrations of power are so intense that they come to dominate the whole social landscape. This power, then, is a general power—rather than a local one—that constructs social reality as such. More-over, it is so pervasive that it is "misrecognized" and thereby legitimized by those subjected to it, who conceal its arbitrari-ness in the process (Couldry 2004). This set of ideas he refers to as "the myth of the mediated center."[4] Simply put, the myth concerns the idea that there is such a thing as the center of society, and that the media represent privileged access to that center. To explain how this concentration of symbolic power in media institutions is maintained, Couldry developed a new approach to media studies, "the media ritual approach." He takes media rituals to be the actions organized around key media-related categories such as liveness, reality, celeb-rity, and so forth. These categories have different reference points to explain why the media are necessary. The live, for instance, suggests that media matter more because they show society's *current* social reality. So although the myth is estab-lished by institutional structures, it is reproduced locally through what people say and do in relation to the media. People, in other words, actively help perpetuate the myth. And since the myth is reproduced on a more general level, there may be skepticism on a local level.

Couldry's main goal, in the early 2000s, was to develop a theory that helped explain media power—not liveness. He focused, therefore, on explaining media power and how live-ness contributed to its reproduction, rather than on providing the means to investigate how liveness is constructed. His definition of liveness was developed in relation to broadcast media, at a time when their symbolic power was largely undisputed. As new forms of liveness emerged based on the internet and digital technologies, they seemed to challenge this concentration of symbolic power. In theory, multiple centers for the production and consumption of symbolic content were made possible since more people had relatively cheap access to media production tools and distribution plat-forms. However, this is not how the situation played out. Social media became the new beneficiaries of a concentration of symbolic power, and they made a claim, like the broadcast media before them, to speak for "us" (Couldry 2014, 619). In 2014 Couldry explored this new configuration as repre-senting a new myth, "the myth of us," which concerns how gatherings on social media are seen as a natural form of collectivity—to the benefit of the bottom line of these platforms. In light of this development in the evolving media landscape, the continued relevance and even intensification of the investment in the category of the live make sense. In this book, my goal is to understand what constitutes liveness, when liveness is and how liveness operates.[5] I would argue, however, that my efforts also contribute to a better understanding of media power, particularly in the social media era. In this context, I disagree with Couldry on the value of Thompson's insights on the workings of power, which in my view should not be discounted—even if certain concentrations of power in the media require that one refer to Bourdieu's work instead. For instance, Thompson's insistence that the different forms of power (he distinguishes four: economic, political, coercive, and symbolic) overlap and shift is a valuable consideration.[6] This makes explicit that symbolic power is connected to other forms of power and cannot be neatly disentangled from it.

When analyzing the particular constellations of liveness of the cases dealt with in this book, I am not attached to a specific function of liveness in advance, nor do I want to fall back on an existing definition built around a particular communication model. Rather, analyzing these constellations will allow me to reformulate the definition of liveness, taking inspiration from the particular situations that apply in each case.

My approach to liveness, then, is distinct from those of others in three main ways. First, my principal aim is to explore the live concept as such: to lay bare how liveness is *constructed around* and *through* media platforms. Specifically, I see liveness as *a socio-technical* construction, a product of a chain of social and technical elements. Second, my approach appreciates that there are multiple constructions of the live, each of which should be valued for its specificity. Analytically speaking, this requires that media platforms should be put to closer scrutiny, and not clustered into generalized groups such as those producing "online liveness" (Couldry 2004) or "digital liveness" (Auslander 2012). Finally, I assume that liveness is subject to a variety of *tensions*: struggles over its meaning among the different actors involved in its construction. Studying such tensions helps to understand the (changing) relations between media institutions and users around media content.

User Participation in the Social Media Era

More than once I have already claimed that the social media era introduces new forms of liveness, but what is "the social media era"? By "social media era" I refer to the period after the dotcom-bubble bust of 2000–2001, a period which has seen an enormous increase in user-generated content and online sharing. This was facilitated by, but is not reducible to, the emergence of social media. Since then, social media are increasingly taken to be replacing broadcast media as the dominant media forms in everyday life.

"Social media," here, refers to

> a group of Internet-based applications that build on the ideological and technological foundations of Web 2.0, and that allow the creation and exchange of user-generated content. (Kaplan and Haenlein 2010, 61)

It was in the wake of the dotcom-bubble bust, at a 2004 conference organized by O'Reilly Media and MediaLive International, that the notion of "Web 2.0" was first explored (O'Reilly 2012).[7] In its most basic definition, Web 2.0 identifies a collection of web technologies that facilitate simple publishing, content sharing, and collaboration. While user-generated content, at the time, was not new, the introduction of easy-to-use interfaces simplified user participation in cultural production. According to Tim O'Reilly, such applications have "a natural architecture of participation" (O'Reilly 2012), meaning that they are systems with a built-in ethic of cooperation, whose services get better as more people use them. Think in this context of how pointless Facebook would be to someone with no "friends." This phenomenon is termed "the network effect," in which social media platforms like Facebook indeed become more valuable as more people use them.   Another core feature of Web 2.0 is its reliance on data management. All these applications are data-driven, which means that in "sharing," "commenting," and "liking" on Facebook, for example, users create data that the platform can monetize.[8] In the social media era, people's relation to and behavior around media content has shifted as new players enter the industry. The debate on the social and cultural effects of social media has bifurcated: utopian discourses on participatory culture on one side, and dystopian discourses on the online economy on the other (Müller 2009). The celebratory perspective takes social media platforms to be vigorous democratizing forces; the critical perspective characterizes our current situation as marked by commercial exploitation through user participation. However, it is arguable that both orientations are equally unable to usefully chart how the relationship between institutions and users has shifted or is currently changing.

The utopian discourse celebrates the social progress made possible through the collective efforts of users (Leadbeater 2009) and is replicated in popular discourses (e.g., in deterministic claims on the role of social media in the Arab Spring uprisings). In a book on corporate strategy, Tapscott and Williams (2010), for instance, have assembled a series of success stories about organizations fostering models of production that are based on community, collaboration, and self-organization. They use these cases to promote user participation in emerging business models, and are convinced that it stimulates social progress. From this perspective, "prosumers," as Alvin Toffler (1990) has called them, are considered to be highly motivated and interested individuals willing to donate their time and energy to a shared cause. Such optimism about participation is also found in the work of Jenkins (2006), though since the mid-2000s he has conceded that in his earlier work, he "underestimated the barriers to achieving what we see as the potential for transformative change emerging as the public has gained greater control over the means of participation" (Jenkins 2014, 7). Nevertheless, he continues to be hopeful about the potential for greater participation through new media. For authors taking a more or less utopian view, the social media era, in any case, has brought closer the possibility of an egalitarian media space, open to mass participation, with multiple centers of production and consumption.

These optimistic claims about participation have been met with criticism, directed not only at the assumed scale on which consumers have been taking on the role of producers (as, in fact, only a small percentage of users actively contribute to and/or produce cultural products) but also at their presumed willingness to collaborate with one another in a community setting marked by shared interests. Another, broadly shared critique is that the stress on the "social" in these accounts hides the commercial character of many of these projects (Schäfer 2011; van Dijck and Nieborg 2009).[9]

Within the dystopian discourse, corporations' dominant role as cultural agent is examined. Authors who take such a view tend to adopt a neo-Marxist perspective, arguing that users are exploited because their "free labor" is capitalized on (Andrejevic 2008; Fuchs 2011; Palmer 2003; Petersen 2008; Scholz 2008; Terranova 2004). Users, they find, are commodified through the sale of their data—or, in a more nuanced version, user labor is implemented into software design (Schäfer 2011).[10] A second strand within the critical discourse on participatory culture is concerned with how these technologies are equally used for control and regulation (Galloway 2006; Morozov 2011; Zittrain 2008). Evgeny Morozov (2011) is exemplary of this group of authors. He has called attention to "the net delusion": the euphoria surrounding the internet, and social media sites in particular, based on the idea that the internet will liberate the world. Morozov debunks this myth by exploring numerous instances in which governments use new media technologies as tools for control and oppression.

Much like the utopian claims ignore some of the realities of participation and its subordination to economic interests, the evaluation of social media platforms from a dystopian perspective ignores the many opportunities provided by new technological frameworks: for example, opportunities to participate in cultural production and in the public sphere at large. In this sense, neither of the two perspectives is optimal in itself. Against the background of these discourses on participation, Jenkins has pointed out:

> It becomes more and more urgent to develop a more refined vocabulary that allows us to better distinguish between models

of participation and evaluate where and how power shifts may be taking place. (Jenkins 2014, 5)

Understanding where and how power shifts would require an analysis of how platforms structure the relations between institutions and users, and of users among themselves. A productive way of considering participation, and with it the relationship between media institutions and users, is to analyze the "space of participation" of media platforms. I explore this concept later in this chapter, as it is instrumental to my analytical approach to liveness. In its relation to media power, deconstructing the live helps to expose the workings of this power.

Analyzing Constellations of Liveness

As I have argued, simply approaching liveness from the perspectives of ontology, phenomenology, or rhetoric is too limiting. To capture its diversity, the live needs to be considered as the product of the complex interaction among institutions, technology, and users. The unique interaction among these three groupings constructs different constellations of live media. As a means to analyze these constellations I draw inspiration from the analytical framework developed to examine participation by Mirko Tobias Schäfer in *Bastard Culture!: How User Participation Transforms Cultural Production* (2011). This framework combines an interest in media *dispositifs* with insights from actor-network theory (ANT) as conducted, most notably, by Michel Callon, Bruno Latour, and John Law. Media *dispositifs*, he explains, refer to the particular setups in which media practices take shape, and they are composed of human and non-human, discursive and non-discursive dimensions. Although authors such as Michel Foucault, Gilles Deleuze, and Hugues Peeters and Philipp Charlier have approached the *dispositif* in different ways, Schäfer contends that they all share the idea that it "describes formations of various participants" (16). In his book he proposes that online participation is shaped at the macro-level by formations of different relations among discourses, technology, and users. These three domains unfold on a micro-level as particular actor networks, as assemblages of human and non-human actors. He uses insights from ANT to trace the connections between actors. This analytical framework, I suggest, is a useful way to approach liveness as well. It enables approaching the live as a construction, one that is reconfigured in different articulations and is shaped by institutions, technologies, and users. In adapting this framework I would propose, however, to jettison the academic baggage of the term *dispositif*. Seeing as Schäfer uses it to refer to formations of various actors, I think calling it a constellation simplifies matters. It conveys the idea of multiple actors coming together as a recognizable form (in my case, the live). Moreover, I refine the three domains of the constellation with slightly different concepts to highlight how institutions, technology, and users interrelate in the construction of the live. Specifically, I opt to refer to the domains in constellations of liveness as metatext, space of participation (Müller 2009), and user responses (van Dijck 2013a).[11] I address each of these in greater depth below.

When studying particular articulations of the live in my case studies, I map the particular actor networks that have unfolded on the micro-level of this constellation (see figure 1). It should be noted that only the actors that act, and thus leave "traces," are analyzed. So although the three domains of liveness are interconnected and together constitute the live, the importance of each domain may vary per constellation. This means that in some cases the metatext might be more formative, while in others it might be the space of participation or user responses. As a result, my discussion of the case studies considers the three domains in different degrees of depth. In assessing how humans and non-human entities interrelate to construct the live, I am influenced by ideas from ANT. For instance, I acknowledge that there are human and non-human actors and that actors acquire agency only in relation to one another. However, my approach deviates from the ANT tradition in two crucial respects. First, my goal is different than ANT's: I aim to produce a theory that explains the phenomenon of liveness. As John Law (2009) reminds us, "Actor network theory is descriptive rather than foundational in explanatory terms" (141). In other words, it is a method aimed at describing. In my research I do not set out

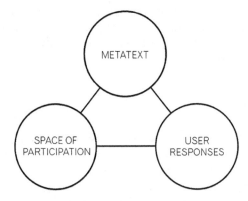

Fig. 1:   A constellation of liveness (figure by Asher Boersma)

to provide non-exhaustive descriptions of networks; rather, I analyze how different actors contribute to constructing the live in particular cases. Thereby I reflect on the conditions and operations of the live. Second, I acknowledge that media "content" is formative to technology and users (van Dijck 2013a)—a fact that ANT tends to overlook.

Before specifying the domains of liveness, an important question remains to be answered: With so many different forms of the live, what bundles them together as a single category? Following Warren Schmaus's (2004) rereading of Durkheim's sociological theory of categories, I find that the meaning of a given category, such as time or space, can be established through its particular social *function*.[12] This sounds more complicated than it is. It simply means that although a category can be constructed in various ways, its function—the role it plays—stays consistent. So although there are multiple forms of the live in the current media landscape, these are bound by the roles they fulfill within it. I speculate, in line with Couldry (2003), that their functions relate to the sustaining of media power.

The Domains of Liveness

My aim, as I have mentioned, is to disclose how liveness is constructed on particular media platforms by examining the interrelated domains of metatext, space of participation, and user responses. Let me offer an explanation of each of these domains to clarify what specifically I am analyzing, beginning with "metatext."

Metatext

The term "paratext" was originally introduced by literary theorist Gérard Genette (1991) to describe features that accompany a text so as to make it present to its readers. Specifically, he meant textual features such as titles, appendices, dedications, and illustrations, which frame the primary text and provide instructions for its reception. As he explains, "The presence surrounding a text of para-textual messages... is not uniformly constant and systematic" (1991, 262). Moreover, "the unequal sense of obligation associated with the paratext is felt by the audience and reader too" (263). This means that not all texts have the same sorts of paratexts and that readers are often acquainted with only a selection of paratexts. Jonathan Gray (2010) has since adapted the concept to make it more suitable for the study of film and television. He considers how a series of media extensions (e.g., opening credit sequences and poster advertisements) creates meaning and establishes relations to upcoming films and television shows, well before they are distributed. These paratexts shape our expectations and understanding of "the text." As Gray puts it:

> Paratexts tell us what to expect, and in doing so, they shape the reading strategies that we will take with us 'into' the text, and they provide the all-important early frameworks through which we will examine, react to, and evaluate textual consumption. (2010, 26)

He adopts the prefix "para-" here, because it highlights that these texts are both distinct from and intrinsically part of the primary text.

What differentiates my use of the term "paratext" from his is my object of study. Rather than film, television, toys, or games, I focus on (social) media platforms. The platforms' paratexts, in my cases, are discursive sites that can be analyzed to disclose how the makers/owners of the platform conceive of its liveness.[13] When analyzing the case studies, I consider the following types of paratexts: information provided on the platform's website, particular features of the platform itself (I specify those in the relevant chapters), promotional materials, press releases, and interviews with representatives of the platform. I am interested in particular in the repetition across these paratexts, as this points to a consistency in ideas about what is "live" about a particular platform. Collectively, these texts are referred to as the *platform metatext*, of which I ask the following question: What do these texts collectively communicate about the meaning of the platform's liveness?

Space of Participation

Significant also is the relation between the metatext and the other two domains, one of which is the space of participation. The concept of "space of participation," introduced by Eggo Müller in his article "Formatted Spaces of Participation: Interactive Television and the Changing Relationship Between Production and Consumption" (2009), helps us to understand how technological, cultural, economic, and legal forces together shape the participatory practices offered by these platforms.[14] In order to critically consider the changing opportunities for participation in participatory culture, Müller uses the concept in a comparative-historical manner. Specifically, he examines how the relationship between production and consumption is structured in the television programs *Aktenzeichen XY* and *Big Brother* and on YouTube. As I am not interested in evaluating participatory culture itself, this comparative dimension is less significant for my research. It does help to shed light on how ways of relating to and around content change the form of liveness. I intend to develop the concept in the following pages, so that it can be used to disclose the participatory practices that specific media platforms offer to their users, and the politics through which this space solidifies. Below, I discuss each of the forces identified by Müller separately. Since he has provided only a basic outline of what they entail, I expand on them, drawing inspiration from the field (among others) of software studies. As technology and society, in my view, are mutually constitutive, I consider technological and cultural forces jointly.[15]

(1) Techno-cultural Forces

The most productive way to consider the constructive role of technologies, I find, is by reflecting on the affordances of the platform's material assemblage, which here also includes software. The term "affordance" was introduced in the work of perceptual psychologist James Gibson (1977), who used the term to discuss the possibilities for action that an environment offers animals (e.g., shelter, fire, water, etc.). The concept gained prominence when Donald Norman (1988) applied it to design theory. Here, the term

> refers to the perceived and actual properties of the thing, primarily those fundamental properties that determine just how the thing could possibly be used. A chair affords ('is for') support and, therefore, affords sitting. A chair can also be carried. Glass is for seeing through, and for breaking. Wood is normally used for solidity, opacity, support, or carving. Flat, porous, smooth surfaces are for writing on. (Norman 1988, 9)

Later, Ian Hutchby (2001) transposed Gibson's concept to another domain, reflecting on the affordances of communication technologies. For Hutchby, the term was valuable in that it facilitated a concern for the technical without slipping into technological determinism. He found that man-made technologies possess both affordances and *constraints*, which are themselves influenced by the materiality of artifacts. As he puts it,

> There is not one but a variety of ways of responding to the range of affordances for action and interaction that a technology presents. We can analyse the development of these responses empirically, but in order to do so we have to accept that technological artefacts do not amount simply to what

their users make of them; what is made of them is accomplished in the interface between human aims and the artefact's affordances. (Hutchby 2001, 453)

Hutchby was critical of authors like Grint and Woolgar (1997), who proposed that technologies should be approached as "texts" that are "written" by their developers, producers, and advertisers, then "read" by consumers. In such an understanding, the text's meaning is negotiated solely by these two parties. The concept of affordance thus helps to draw attention to the role of the material aspects of things in constraining the possible meanings and uses of technology. Affordances arise from an object's material properties and its design (Hutchby 2001; Norman 1988; Schäfer 2011).

In analyzing how technological forces shape participation on platforms, Müller chiefly focuses on the *user interface*. He does not, however, provide any analytical tools with which to address the technological dimension below the visible user interface. Inspired by the interdisciplinary research field of software studies, I find it necessary, in the case of online social media platforms, to include reflections on the *algorithms* and *protocols* that process and channel these platforms' (meta) data. Data (i.e., text, image, sound) and metadata (data about data) are resources for coding technologies (van Dijck 2013a). Algorithms process data: they are the set of instructions a machine uses to calculate a given task. For instance, Netflix, a popular on-demand streaming media platform, uses an algorithm to recommend movies and shows to its users based on calculations involving (meta)data, including the browsing and purchasing behavior of all its subscribers, which it uses to establish relations between user tastes and preferences. Protocols, on the other hand, are rules for regulating the transmission and exchange of messages in distributed networks. They essentially control data flow. Both algorithms and protocols, Bucher has pointed out,

are important elements when considering networked and software-enabled media such as social networking sites, as they in many respects prescribe and define the possible actions within these programmed spaces. (2012, 17)

User interface, algorithms, and protocols each introduce different platform affordances and constraints, and thus shape the space of participation.[16]

In addition to the platforms' material affordances and constraints, their implicit rules and conventions (as opposed to explicit rules found in Terms of Use, e.g.) equally shape their use. These rules and conventions are established through the recurring practices of a platform's users. To clarify this, Müller offers an example of user practice on YouTube, where the informality of the comments on video-sharing sites reflects everyday language. In other words, this style of communication was established as a norm through the practices that emerged on the platform.

(2) Economic Forces

Economic forces also exert an impact on a platform's space of participation. I would argue that two main economic forces construct the possible range and forms of participation on a platform. These concern, respectively, the imperative of its business model and the costs that users incur through platform use. Rather than seeking to produce audiences to be sold to advertisers (Smythe 1977), as in broadcast television, online platforms have given rise to new business models. While most online platforms currently generate value out of user-generated data, their business models range in nature and complexity. Google, for instance, sells keywords, statistics about keywords, and search results through its AdSense program. In doing so, the corporation acts simultaneously as an advertising agency, ratings company, and content provider (Lee 2011). The possibilities of interaction afforded by the platform through its design support these business principles. Different business models are immediately evident when comparing my case studies. Whereas the online music-collaboration platform eJamming sells a service to its users (i.e., access to software and tools that enable online jamming with others), the situation for *The Voice* is more akin to Dallas Smythe's (1977) contention that mass media sell audiences to advertisers. In the case of Facebook also, audiences are sold to advertisers—although other principles are also adhered to here. According to Jenkins, the platform "seek[s] to capture, commodify and control the public's desire for meaningful participation" (Jenkins 2014, 10). Moreover, to be able to use social media platforms, users must also take on certain costs—and these need to be taken into account. Such costs include expenditure for computer equipment (with particular hardware and software specifications), broadband connectivity, and/or specific online services (e.g., subscription fees).

(3) Legal Forces

Finally, legal concerns warrant some reflection on the explicit rules concerning property, privacy, and acceptable behavior on a given platform (van Dijck 2013a). These are often formulated in EULAs (End-User License Agreements) and Terms of Use (including community guidelines). By signing off on these "contracts," users agree to particular uses of the platform and potentially face legal action if they are in breach of said rules. They place constraints on, for instance, who uses the platform (e.g., one must be age thirteen years or over to sign up for Instagram and Facebook, among other social networks) and how it is used (e.g., copyright law prevents certain content from being shared legally online).

User Responses

Along with the metatext and the space of participation, "user responses," as Van Dijck (2013a) calls them, play a role in the construction of liveness. These responses are instances of reflection and commentary on the platform by the users themselves. Van Dijck explores such user responses in order to disclose the norms and values associated with social media platforms. My contention here is that they can also be studied to establish how users understand a platform's liveness. When users become critical of the understanding of liveness put forth by the metatext, they respond either by appropriating the platform itself, changing its scripted use, or by publicly articulating their dissatisfaction (e.g., on a page, forum, blog, or via tweets). When analyzing my case studies, I am interested specifically in what people *explicitly* say and do (so to a certain extent, I am also looking at practices here) that reflects on the *meaning* and *value* of liveness on the platform. In other words, I do not consider such user responses so as to establish how people experience these media platforms, but only for what this type of user agency contributes to the meaning of "live," and insofar as this exposes how users understand the liveness proposed by the metatext. In some cases, the amount of user responses available for consideration will be limited. This does not, however, detract from their capacity to further our understanding of the liveness of the platform.

3
Liveness and Institutionalization

According to Paddy Scannell (2001; 2014), people can have authentic experiences of events—experiences that are entirely their own—by watching them on television. Live television, he claims, creates "possibilities of participation, effects of being-there, in ways that entitle people to claim the viewing of an event as an entitlement to an experience" (Scannell 2001, 409). Television's communicative structure makes a particular world available to everyone in the same way, but that world also becomes part of the everyday life and experience of individuals. Viewers can therefore claim to have had an experience of that event and can discuss it with others who have seen it too.

Although live broadcasts are conceived as being "naturally" available to all, they are carefully produced and managed to realize their producers' intentions. The liveness of broadcasts, Scannell claims, "is the worked at, achieved and accomplished effect of the human application and use of technologies whose ontological characteristic is immediate connectivity" (Scannell 2014, 99). However, the labor processes that inform program output (e.g., the structuring of program components into a narrative, or the switching between multiple camera positions), the so-called "care structures," are hidden. We take them for granted because, precisely, they allow us to take them for granted. To further clarify that liveness is not a natural fact but rather something that is worked at, Scannell invokes the surveillance camera. "What it records," he points out, "has the quality of immediacy, not of liveness. It produces a visual record, but not one that is watchable" (2014, 98). To create the effect of liveness, human intervention is needed.

While Scannell makes valuable contributions to our thinking about the live, my take on these matters differs in two respects. First, the live, in my account, is not just the product of the media's care structures but is a construction that emerges from (media) institutions, and also technologies and users—and, specifically, the interactions between them. Like Scannell, however, I believe this construction is taken for granted and hidden from view. The inherent contradiction here, between liveness as a construction and its perception as being somehow "natural," is what I call in this book the "paradox of liveness." Second, Scannell's approach also overlooks the issue of power, which I believe liveness is entangled with. In my view, Scannell's phenomenological perspective can usefully be complemented with insights from Couldry's ideological perspective. As I mentioned in chapter 2, liveness helps to sustain existing power relations.

Here in this chapter, I consider the relation between liveness and institutionalization, as a means to tease out the "paradox of liveness." This relation helps to explain why broadcasters need to "work at" content to make it appealing for viewing, and draws attention to the resources required for this purpose. In what follows, I examine the live-streaming video platform Livestream, which, upon revamping itself in 2011, provocatively claimed to have redefined the live. It did so, specifically, after transitioning from a platform for user-generated content to one more focused on professionally produced content. By comparing the constellations for live-streaming on the before-and-after versions of the platform, I can reflect on the link between liveness and institutionalization.

The Mogulus/Original Livestream Metatext: Emulating Broadcast TV

Livestream was launched under the name Mogulus in 2007, a year in which several live video sites debuted, including

Justin.tv, BlogTV, and Ustream.tv. To reveal how the meaning of the live is constructed on such a platform, I discuss this platform's metatext, space of participation, and user responses. In doing so, I show that these domains construct the platform's liveness with explicit reference to ideas of broadcast TV. My assumption here is that the site's "trial phase," which lasted roughly from the platform's inception in 2007 to 2011, can be approached (its name change notwithstanding) as a single constellation of liveness. The identity and form of the platform remained quite stable between Mogulus and what, retrospectively, came to be known as the "Original" Livestream. However, even some of the smaller tweaks and expansions that were made in the shift from Mogulus to the site's first iteration under the name Livestream are interesting, in that this gradual transition prepared the platform for its later, more fundamental transformation from a service aimed at video bloggers and their viewers to one targeting a more professional group of content producers and consumers.

To understand why the company behind Mogulus ventured into live-streaming, and to trace how the metatext framed the liveness of the platform, I start by reflecting on an interview with Max Haot, co-founder and CEO of Mogulus/Livestream, on the day after the platform was officially launched. I complement the insights yielded by this interview with an analysis of the platform's website as it developed between 2007 and 2011, using snapshots archived by the Wayback Machine of the Internet Archive. In addition, I also use press releases written for the launch and consider the composition and layout of the platform itself.

In "Mogulus" (2007), an online video interview with Jamison Tilsner of Tilzy.TV, Haot stated that other live-streaming platforms were boring, because they only offered footage from a single, often stationary, camera. Mogulus, he explained, challenged itself to change the image of live-streaming and make it more interesting. To achieve this goal, it provided numerous creator tools that expanded the traditional methods of live-streaming. It added a way for users to switch between multiple real-time cameras (including mobile phones) during a broadcast, introduced overlay graphics, and included a video library. These features helped users mix recorded content with real-time camera footage. Mogulus's press materials, touting the rationale behind these tools,

Fig. 2:   A snapshot of the Mogulus home page (on August 20, 2007, via the Wayback Machine)

claimed that they were giving ordinary people the means to operate their own television station and to do all the things a television producer could.

Reflecting on the video library, Haot commented that he thought it more important to offer content in a linear fashion than to broadcast such content "live" (i.e., as it happened). Data gathered by Mogulus, he said, had indicated that linear programming was good for audience retention, helping to expose viewers to new content and creating the illusion of a continuous stream of fresh content. The company concluded that viewers spent more time watching live-streaming channels that offered a constant flow of content than those that featured videos on demand.

The Internet Archive's Wayback Machine allows one to examine snapshots of the company's web pages as they looked in 2007. Figure 2 is a snapshot of the website as it was set up on August 20, two months before the platform's public launch. It reveals the company's ambition of enabling user-generated "television stations." This is apparent in the original tagline for Mogulus.com: "Mogulus gives you everything you need to launch your own LIVE 24/7 television station." It is also made clear in the main text. Perhaps most striking here is how "yesterday" is juxtaposed with today. (Something similar happens on the site's "About Us" page, where graphics show yesterday's tools—the television control room, video-switching hardware, and a character generator—alongside analogous contemporary tools in the Mogulus studio.) This way, the state of affairs in the past, when the media landscape was dominated by an institutional "center" with a concentration of symbolic resources, is shown to be discontinuous with the present situation, with its burgeoning possibilities for multiple centers of production and consumption to emerge. In other words, this fosters the idea that the internet does—thanks to Mogulus—disrupt media power.

The Mogulus website, at this stage, calls the platform "a revolution in live television." This same idea is expressed in the subtitle to the "About Us" button, which also provides a link to the Mogulus manifesto, and in a video uploaded to YouTube in 2007 that explains how the platform works.[17] This way, the new service emphasized its role in redistributing agency, by giving individuals the tools to produce and broadcast content. The main message here was that, as long as a user had a webcam and access to the internet, Mogulus could make broadcasting widely accessible to the public.

With a rhetoric similar to that of social media applications in general, Mogulus characterized the barrier to participation as being very low. Realizing the equivalent of a television station was said to be as easy as clicking the "Apply for Beta" button. In fact, the portmanteau "Mogul-us" reflects this rather utopian ideal of democratizing the broadcast-television paradigm, by playing with the notion that anyone can be a media mogul. However, some conflict arises here, as the platform's promise also centers on the possibility that what gets broadcast is no longer determined by such "moguls." Transforming the user into a mogul, indeed, allows that user to appropriate the power that comes with being one.

The early Mogulus metatext persistently compared live-streaming to live-broadcasting. Insofar as it concerns the term "live," the concept is perhaps addressed most directly in the website's FAQ, which once again likens the liveness of live-streaming to that found in broadcast television. The comparison here also has a technological dimension, as the site claims that Mogulus is able to offer liveness by eliminating the common twenty-second delay in live-streaming. The near instantaneity of its stream, it adds, allows the viewer to experience what the producer has put on the air "in less than one second." Here we see that liveness is also about making connections—in this case, connecting producers with viewers. Arguably, the assumption is made that by focusing on the same content simultaneously, both parties can construct a shared frame of reference. Liveness, in other words, is seen to have a social dimension.

Liveness in this sense, however, is not what is chiefly highlighted on the 2007 Mogulus website. At the time, the metatext suggested that the platform mimicked the medium of television primarily in two ways: (a) by offering users the tools to produce a *linear* viewing experience, and (b) by allowing them to *mix* "live" and recorded content. Recall in this context Haot's claims about the company's attempts to differentiate itself from other live-streaming platforms by ridding live-streaming of its "boring" reputation. As the Mogulus homepage emphasized,

> With Mogulus, you can blend your webcam, video clips from YouTube, and your own original content into your own unique TV program.... When you're not broadcasting live, turn on the auto-pilot and let it drive your playlist.

As I mentioned, linear programming was emphasized, according to CEO Haot, because it could ensure audience retention: even after a live broadcast, prerecorded material could keep viewers entertained on the channel.[18]

By mid-2008, there was a noticeable shift in the narrative presented on Mogulus's website. More—and different— parties were being identified for whom the platform would be suitable. At the time, the following blurb was posted on the homepage:

> Whether you are a video blogger, independent producer or large media company, there's a Mogulus for you. Click here to get started!

This shift might be explained by the investment, in July 2008, of $10 million in the live-streaming service by the Gannett Company, Inc., which was using the Mogulus tools for several of its newspapers (including *USA Today*), television networks, and radio stations. Shortly afterward the financial sector crashed, which prompted Mogulus to begin deploying and monetizing premium business (TechCrunch 2011). To do so, the company found it necessary to rebrand itself. In May 2009 it presented its features under a different look and name. Specifically, it changed its name to Livestream, hoping the platform would now become synonymous with live-streaming to a greater extent than it had before (Parr 2009). In the years following the platform's renaming, the company continued to compare its live-streaming to traditional TV. In the product tour offered on its 2011 website, for instance, it used slogans such as "Just like you see on television," "Just like traditional TV," and "Like any multi-million dollar studio."

The organization of the platform's "channels" also highlights its connection with traditional broadcast TV, and offers some additional insights in relation to the live. In 2007, the platform started out with a "Mogulus Grid" on its homepage. This video wall showed the twenty-six most popular Mogulus channels simultaneously and had an integrated chat feature. It also included a program guide to search/browse channels not shown on the Grid. In late January 2008, a list of channel categories was added, and by the first week of December 2008 the Grid had been removed. The switch between these two features, one might argue in retrospect, points to the platform's transformation into a service that primarily offers professional content, made more accessible through enhanced navigational tools. The different layouts that the website experimented with in the period up to 2008, moreover, reflect a particular interest in its "Live Now" channels. Through the placement of categories, a hierarchy was created wherein "Live Now" content was privileged over all other kinds. In this respect, too, a shift was already taking place before the platform was renamed.

The look of the Livestream platform in 2009, which I refer to in what follows as the "Original" Livestream, was more streamlined than in its earlier iteration as Mogulus. Rather than presenting a single long list of categories, it now selected top categories that expanded into dropdown menus. In addition to "Live Now," these top categories included "News," "Entertainment," "Music," "Sports," "Games," and "Xfire Games." The presence of these categories, I would argue, supports the idea that the platform was positioning itself as an analogue of traditional television, as opposed to other online video platforms such as YouTube (on demand) and Ustream (live).

One category featured on the Mogulus and the Original Livestream platforms, however, was something one wouldn't find on traditional television: the "Lifecasting" section. This term refers to a genre of online video that presents the continuous real-time broadcast of one's life through first-person video. In addition, Original Livestream introduced its "Games" and "Xfire Games" categories. Both refer to channels where gamers could share their gameplay with others. Although the games categories can also be found on traditional television, they are not principal categories there. Their dominance on the Mogulus/Original Livestream platform makes them essential contributors to the meaning of live-streaming within the particular constellation I am discussing. Both categories reaffirm how the liveness in this constellation represented a space where amateurs—pointedly, *not* professionals—could broadcast their content, in spite of the smaller shifts toward different kinds of users (indeed, professional users) that are also noticeable in retrospect. In addition, such categories as "Live Now" and "Lifecasting" point to an emerging trend that highlights and, by the same token, places extra value on, "live" content (i.e., content recorded and broadcast simultaneously).

The Space of Participation

I now redirect my attention from the metatext (to which I return below) and move on to sketching the space of participation on the Mogulus and the Original Livestream platforms. In doing so, I aim to investigate their design and what they afforded to their users. I begin by comparing the basic interfaces of a few live-streaming platforms (not only Mogulus and Original Livestream, but also Ustream and the now defunct Justin.tv) to that of the on-demand streaming platform YouTube. The goal of this comparison is twofold. First, it helps provide a basic outline of the space of participation offered viewers by the Mogulus and the Original Livestream platforms. Second, the comparison foregrounds the seemingly inextricable relation on streaming platforms between the live transmission of content and real-time socialization. I explore this relation to reflect on the connection between liveness and interactivity.

Between Live-streaming and On-demand Platforms

When considering more generally the respective spaces of participation that characterize live-streaming and on-demand streaming platforms, focusing on how they are used to view—rather than to produce—content, a couple of common features are immediately noticeable. To begin with, both sorts of platforms give users the option to share video content either through Facebook, Twitter, etc., or via the copying of an embed code or a hyperlink. Furthermore, they allow for content to be "liked" and for the user to make recommendations as to what other content viewers are likely to enjoy, based on the viewing and browsing behaviors of platform users.

There are also several obvious differences between the two types of platforms. First, live-streaming platforms all note how many viewers are watching content *now*. This was true not only for the Mogulus and the Original Livestream platforms, but also for Ustream and Justin.tv. In this respect, they differ from YouTube, which lists the total amount of views over time. This quick comparison, I would argue, suggests that simultaneous viewing is considered an important dimension of the live-streaming experience.

Another difference, related to the first, is that live-streaming platforms offer chat modules that facilitate real-time interaction among viewers. They also encourage their viewers to log on to Facebook and Twitter, allowing them to participate in an online conversation and providing a timeline of the comments made on these social networks. By contrast, YouTube, as an on-demand streaming platform, provides a space where users can leave comments. These comments are dated and time-stamped. It is interesting to note here that YouTube Live, the YouTube platform for streaming live events, includes a counter showing how many people are watching *now*, as well as a chat module.

The distinction between these two types of streaming platforms suggests a "natural" relation between live transmission and real-time social interactions. This observation relates to an insight by Couldry, who argues that interactivity around content is a means of "showing, in performance, the otherwise merely assumed connection between medium and representative social group" (2003, 109). Understood in this way, the view-counter and chat module fuel the idea of collective viewing, offering users the possibility of being "a part of" the event by discussing it with others as it unfolds. It also suggests that the content is important and must be seen *now* rather than later. Of course, in the event of a failure to capture continuous activity, this "strategy" could easily backfire, as it would highlight the fact that no one is watching.

Creator Tools

Aside from the viewers' space of participation, another space of participation is relevant here: the space occupied by producers, emerging on both the Mogulus and the Original Livestream platforms in relation to the creator tools the site made available to its users, which allowed for the production and distribution of video content.[19] Here, too, we find techno-cultural, economic, and legal forces at work that shape how content can be produced and distributed.

For those working with these creator tools at the time, the primary techno-cultural factor influencing production and distribution was the recommended 700 kbps minimum upstream bandwidth, which ensured high-quality video streaming.[20] Given that in 2010 the average upload speed in the United States was 595 kbps ("Report on Internet Speeds" 2010), one might well ask how many people could actually use the platform the way it was intended. It can be argued, then, that the company was probably targeting a tech-savvy crowd, thus contradicting its claim to democratize television. As Mogulus, the platform offered a single tool to produce a live broadcast through Mogulus Studio (a browser-based encoder). Eventually, as (Original) Livestream, it added two more creator tools: Webcaster (a browser-based application) and Procaster (a web-based application). Before addressing what each tool could do, I should point out that all three methods allowed producers to chat with viewers through a chat client, and enabled the sending of tweets from within the application.

Mogulus Studio was the first and most expansive of the tools, and the only one available in 2007. Following the platform's rebranding, it was renamed "Livestream Studio." The tool enabled the real-time mixing of graphics, videos, and webcam footage; it also allowed producers to enter a text graphic in the lower third of the video content or to create a text crawl. What set Livestream Studio apart from Webcaster and Procaster is that it featured an autopilot function (where users could queue storyboards and files to play when not broadcasting live content) and offered tools to manage a public video-on-demand library. Here users could store videos that had either been uploaded or imported from podcasts, webservers, or a YouTube account. The Livestream Studio also enabled users to work with multiple cameras. As a multi-user application, it facilitated collaboration among multiple producers, possibly even scattered across the globe, in real time. As I indicated earlier, at the time the platform's metatext stressed how users could assume the position of television moguls, by employing creator tools that referenced traditional television practices and curated linear programming. The autopilot feature, available in Livestream Studio, can be seen as the materialization of this ambition. It enabled producers to broadcast to audiences even when they were not live.

By contrast, Procaster and Webcaster, both made available in 2009, were fairly simple tools that allowed users to set up a live broadcast in minutes.[21] Procaster was encoding software that needed to be downloaded and installed. However, certain system requirements had to be met for installation, so the software was not available to all users.[22] With the Procaster software, users could encode settings as well as the input sources for video and audio. In addition, they could stream "live" from a cell phone or video camera, and were offered a selection of settings for the broadcast: Game Mode, Screen Mode, or 3D Mix. The Game Mode option enabled users to broadcast gameplay at full frame rate, though this was available only to Windows (and not Mac or Linux) users. Users could also screencast from their computers in 2D Mix or 3D Mix. Whereas 2D Mix displayed the secondary screen in the bottom left corner of the screen, the 3D Mix option displayed the secondary video source next to the full screen-capture window.

Webcaster was a web-based application intended to serve as "a simplified web-based version of Procaster," allowing users to record their broadcasts and import the completed recordings into a record section, added to the autopilot or on-demand libraries. Additionally, next to the text monitor, users could select one of three options: "local," "remote" or "off." Selecting "local" allowed them to see the direct camera feed. With "remote" they could see what was being broadcast on the channel where they were broadcasting. The "off" option simply turned the monitor off.

Each of these three tools changed how content could be produced and distributed via the platform. In affording and constraining broadcast production capabilities in different ways, each contributed to the meaning of the platform's liveness. Whereas Procaster, for instance, enabled streaming gameplay, the Livestream Studio facilitated a more complex mixing of graphics, webcam videos and prerecorded footage. However, these tools can all be seen as part of the company's desire to subsume live-streaming into a linear-programming paradigm.

The Challenges of Monetization

With regard to the economic forces shaping the space of participation, Mogulus/Livestream has experimented with different ways of securing a revenue stream. In its early days, Mogulus worked with overlay advertising. Then, in December 2008, it adopted a freemium business model: it offered the service for free, but charged for a package of "premium" features (Hopkins 2008). By 2011 it had diversified these premium features, providing several different pricing options for the Original Livestream platform. These I discuss presently, but here I highlight the main challenges facing live-streaming platforms that are centered on the hosting of user-generated content (UGC), by relating this orientation briefly to You-Tube's "wait-and-see" approach toward live-streaming.

Nicholas Carlson (2008) connected YouTube's hesitance to offer live-streaming—which, however, it has now ventured into—to two interrelated problems pertaining to monetization. The first is the companies' unwillingness to advertise next to user-generated content (Kim 2012). They are afraid of losing control over what their brand might be associated with, as this could lead to undesirable juxtapositions (e.g., a campaign banner against underage drinking would have its message undercut if placed near a video showing a group of intoxicated teenagers). By contrast, mainstream media formats have successfully co-evolved to meet the demands of advertising and even reinforce its messages (Andrejevic 2009).

The problem of "uncontrollable users," in fact, plagues all platforms hosting user-generated content (Carlson 2008). In opening up to user contributions, a platform can be used for the sharing of indecent and copyrighted materials. The question that has emerged as a result of such illegal practices, and which has played out in court, is who can and should be held accountable for what is shared on these platforms. In a producer-controlled space, such as the kind created in traditional television, it is simple to determine who is responsible for what is broadcast. The matter, however, becomes more complex with platforms that host materials from millions of individual producers, who upload content from around the globe.

The Digital Millennium Copyright Act (DMCA), a 1998 U.S. law, protects service providers, specifically, from legal action due to the copyright violations committed by their platforms' users. However, the law does mandate that service providers remove infringing material within twenty-four hours after receiving a legitimate takedown notice from rights' holders. For live-streaming platforms, where videos are produced, distributed, and primarily consumed as an event unfolds, such a removal window makes little sense (as most potential viewers would already have watched the stream by the time it is removed). Whereas on-demand video platforms can remove content when the copyright holder files a complaint, or track infringing materials through filtering technologies, the timeframe in which to act on copyright infringement is problematic for live video content. For a platform such as Livestream, this makes the monitoring of user content even more pressing than for a website like YouTube. Live content requires an automatic takedown system that allows rights holders to kill streams without having to send takedown notices. This demands a more active role on the part of the platform in the prevention of copyright infringement.

Livestream has wanted to retain the free model made possible by advertisements, keeping the platform open to user-generated content while concurrently trying to prevent advertisements from accompanying illegal or indecent content. To this end, the company has enacted what it called a "zero tolerance policy" for piracy and other such matters. To efficiently monitor the platform for, among other things, copyright breaches, it selectively focused on channels that attracted more than fifty concurrent viewers. This meant that rather than having to filter through millions of channels, it only had to monitor several thousand.

As of February 2009, Livestream users with a free channel were limited to fifty concurrent viewers for as long as their channel remained unverified. In addition, free channels were not mentioned in the platform channel guide. For these restrictions to be lifted, users could request channel verification, which was provided free of charge. The verification process required that users submit a short text to explain what they intended to use the channel for. This way, the platform could claim to have been misled by a channel user in the event of some kind of infringement. Arguably, then, Livestream exchanged its proactive stance for a defensive approach to illegal practices or obscenity.

The second challenge that Carlson claims prevented YouTube from joining the live-stream bandwagon early on is the overhead expense of live-streaming. He observes:

Live streaming is very expensive and hard to monetize.... If just 10% of YouTube's users adopted live streaming, bandwidth costs would go up 20% to 25%. That's because live streaming clips tend to last much longer than the short video clips typical of YouTube. (Carlson 2008, n.p.)

Despite the relatively high costs of bandwidth for live-streaming compared to on-demand platforms, Haot has defended live-streaming as a profitable business, citing the duration of the average viewing session on the Livestream network, which as of 2011 lasted somewhere around sixteen minutes and was similar to that of Hulu, which features long video forms. By comparison, the average session on YouTube at that time was only around three to four minutes (Beet.TV 2011).[23] It is unclear, however, whether monetizing longer viewer sessions is in fact sustainably profitable and whether its returns offset the higher costs of hosting live streams.

Nevertheless, offering live-streaming for "free" to users makes it difficult to contain the costs of bandwidth, and this has to be compensated for in some way. As I mentioned, at first Mogulus offered free use of its services, but with overlay advertising. Later, in 2008, it switched to a freemium business model, in which the "Pro" account provided expanded features and the possibility of removing advertisements. Just before it was revamped as "the New Livestream" in late 2011, the (Original) Livestream platform offered three different plans: a "free" plan, a "channel" plan, and a "network" plan. These plans corresponded to the three types of users the platform targeted: individuals, professionals, and organizations. It wasn't until 2011 that Livestream broke even for the first time (TechCrunch 2011).

The "free" plan offered users unlimited free channels, ad-supported streaming, SD quality, and a ten GB storage limit. For an annual fee of $3,500 it was possible to upgrade to a "channel" plan that provided one premium channel, including 3,000 viewer hours, 1,000 GB of storage, and HD quality streams. The "network" plan cost $12,500 per year. It featured ten premium channels with 15,000 viewer hours and the same amount of storage and video quality given to subscribers of the premium "channel" plan. The premium plans and third-party investments made the free plan possible.

Aside from offering more storage space, the channel plan and the network plan allowed producers to remove Livestream branding and to monetize content through advertising. By this stage it should be clear that the three plans each afforded and constrained what was possible with broadcasting in different ways. The differences revolved around price, advertisements, amount of possible viewers, quality of the transmitted video, and available storage capacity. Basically, the more people willing to pay for the service, the more they could do with the channel, both qualitatively and quantitatively.

User Responses: Unattractive User-generated Channels

Having examined both the metatext and the space of participation, I now take a closer look at user comments during the 2007–2011 period, in order to sketch a more complete picture of how the live is constructed on this live-streaming platform. In addition, I also consider some aspects of user practice. Here, I focus specifically on the channels that were listed in the channel guide (in practice, at least as of February 2009, all channels that likely attracted more than fifty concurrent viewers).[24]

The Livestream forum provided users a space to pose questions about how the platform worked and raise problems they encountered in working with the software or in hooking up hardware (e.g., cameras and microphones). Several discussions took place here on copyright issues; in particular, questions about what constitutes a copyright violation. With respect to liveness, there was one question, raised by two different users, that helps to provide insight into how users understood the live in live-streaming.[25] Both asked how they could identify whether the video being streamed on a channel was in fact "live." Animemog, for one, made the following comment:

> Sorry for being a bit of a newb, but how do I know if a channel is live or showing a pre-record? I've watched some

streams with a decent amount of people and then the video
will seamlessly change and then I realize it's not live at all.
And when it is pre-recorded, I don't know which video it's
playing from the playlist.[26]

Frank Adams raised the following question:

> I am watching a whole series of streams. Some of them are
> live, others are recorded and replays. Is there any way to tell
> which ones are live and which are replays?[27]

Livestream Support replied to these questions with the following answer: "A feed that is broadcasting live will say
'LIVE' next to the pause button on the bottom left corner of
the player."

Upon playing around with the options myself, however, I
noticed that the chromo key that identified supposedly live
broadcasts was featured among others in content such as
music videos. The red icon labeling the material as "live"
would disappear only if the video was loaded from the
channel library. (So, incidentally, did the counter which kept
track of how many people were watching the content at a
given point—which is interesting in light of my comparison
of the spaces of participation of live-streaming and on-demand
video platforms.) It seems, then, that there was a misunderstanding between tech support and users over the point of
reference for the "live" in live-streaming. Whereas the answer
of the former referred to the status of transmission, the
viewers had actually asked how to distinguish between prerecorded content and content broadcast at the time of its
recording (the latter group's implicit definition of "live" in
this instance). In this particular case, the difference in inter-
pretations seems to have been the result of other points of
reference. In chapter 5, I return to the importance of contextualizing the live.

User practice can also indicate how people respond to
what live-streaming platforms can offer. In my analysis here,
as I have mentioned, I focus on the channels officially listed
in the Livestream channel guide. By 2010, most of these channels showed footage broadcast/streamed by name brands,
event organizers (e.g., concerts from popular bands such as
Foo Fighters), or small media institutions (e.g., a live video

stream of a DJ at work, produced by a local radio station), high schools, or universities.[28] The pervasiveness of professional and semi-professional content in the listings certainly suggests that established institutions are better able to provide content and attract viewers than individual users are. Statements from platform founder Haot in an interview with *Inc. com* in 2013 support this observation. The piece contains several reflections on how individuals used the platform and on the problems they faced when running their own channels. Haot remarked:

> We were seeing bloggers starting to use [Mogulus] and then they would stop using it because they didn't have the content, they didn't have the audience, they didn't have the know-how. But then we found event owners were starting to use our service. And then we would see that at bigger audience [*sic*], the content was more compelling because it's an event. It's already there, you just capture the event. (Maclean 2013, n.p.)[29]

According to this logic, people simply weren't watching content produced and broadcast by individual users (i.e., those not affiliated with a larger organization or event). Such content was thereby caught in a self-perpetuating cycle: as its lack of attention decreased its visibility on the website, it had little opportunity to attract more viewers. Events, in contrast, appeared in the listings *because* they had viewers, and in this way could attract even more.

In exploring the constellation of liveness for the Mogulus/ Original Livestream platform, I have begun to show how liveness took shape there, and offered some insights on the nature ("meaning") of liveness as constructed within this particular constellation. Between 2007 and 2011, the company behind the platform was in a trial phase, still experimenting with ways to make it catch on. From its inception, the tools it made available to producers supported a "new" conception of live-streaming—one that no longer made its user bound to a single (web)camera and allowed for continuous broadcasting via a mix of recorded and "live" content. The sort of live-streaming stimulated in this way borrowed heavily from a particular conception of broadcast television, which involved production tools that facilitated the use of multiple cameras, allowed the addition of text overlays and a crawl, and could create linear programming through a mix of live and non-live material.

Yet even though the conception of liveness in the Mogulus/ Original Livestream constellation borrowed heavily from notions associated with traditional television, the platform also allowed room to refashion broadcasting. This is evident, for instance, in the emergence of new cultural practices (like "homecasting" [van Dijck 2007]) and cultural forms (e.g., game casting) on the live-streaming platform, due to the opportunity given viewers to produce their own content. At the same time, offline practices such as recording gameplay and keeping a diary have acquired online counterparts on Livestream. All these genres are less common in broadcast television.

Viewers engaged with video content on the Original Livestream platform in many ways that were similar to watching content on a traditional television set. Even the chat function and "Share" and "Like" buttons enabled practices that resemble existing offline practices—workplace water-cooler conversations about the previous day's broadcast, the lending of tapes, or the making of viewer recommendations to others. What differentiates live-streaming platforms here is not only that the television production process has been drastically simplified in that, theoretically at least, it involves far less specialized know-how, but also that many people can now financially afford to create something akin to a television channel for themselves, without having to purchase expensive equipment for production and distribution.

In the end, the platform put an interesting spin on liveness by offering audiences a very different relation to content than they had been accustomed to. Rather than the *user relation to liveness*, which viewers were familiar with from the broadcast-television model (where content was "pushed" "at" them), users could now enter a *producer relation to liveness*, in that they could broadcast content themselves. (In chapter 6, this topic is explored further, using the example of the social network site Facebook.) However, as the account given here shows, the first version of the platform to a certain extent failed to realize its ambitions. Even though it was successful in lowering the threshold for television production and distribution, few individuals seem to have had the ready content or expertise to run a channel—or at the very least, to amass an audience for it. Phrasing it in terms of liveness, one could argue that these individual users failed to deliver "live" content—in the qualitative sense, as the kind of content that a professional live broadcast would offer. In light of Scannell's observation that a lot of unseen hard work goes into program output, we might attribute this to the fact that not everyone is in a position to invest/produce so much work.

The New Livestream Metatext: Being There

Let us move on from the Mogulus/Original Livestream constellation to what took shape upon the launch of the next version of Livestream. Zooming in on the example of the Volvo Ocean Race, an event that took place from October 2011 to July 2012, below I reflect further on why the platform needed to target a new user base. Having been specifically selected by the company to showcase the new platform's features and overall identity, the event is interesting in terms of how a new constellation of liveness came about.

By late 2011, Livestream had built a new platform, introduced to the world as "the New Livestream." Around this time, CEO Haot, in an interview with *TechCrunch*, elaborated why such a step was necessary (TechCrunch 2011). He claimed that although his product (a live-streaming platform) had been a good idea from the start, the vision that had accompanied it—aiming to democratize broadcast television—had been misguided. During the platform's trial phase, it had become clear that live-streamed events attracted far larger audiences than user channels ever would. The company therefore slowly started to shift its attention to the "event television" market and began specializing in tools that allowed event owners to broadcast live and engage with their audiences.

With the New Livestream rollout, the metatext and space of participation of the platform were fundamentally modified, producing a new constellation for live-streaming. This break with the old was made very explicit in the provocative slogan that accompanied the new platform: "Live. Redefined." The company's mission statement now stated that its goal was

> to provide the premiere interactive live streaming platform for every event owner, broadcaster and premium rights holder in the music, movie, newspaper, radio and television industries.

To more precisely locate the shift in how the company framed the "live" in live-streaming, accessing snapshots of Livestream's prior web pages with the aid of the Wayback Machine is helpful once again. Doing so reveals that a subtle change was made to the main webpage title, somewhere between late August and early September 2010. At this time, the tagline was changed from "Livestream—Broadcast Live streaming video" to "BE THERE." I see in this revision a clear indication that the platform was now being promoted to users as a way to be a part of an event, by watching and engaging with channels—rather than as an opportunity for users to start channels of their own (as was the case with the Original Livestream platform). This shift in the company's strategy, which involved targeting viewers as users but event owners as clients, became more visible with the new website in 2012. At this point in time the visitor, rather than being invited to "Broadcast Now" when accessing the website, was summoned to "Discover & Experience Live Events."

Production quality varied for the live-streaming events aggregated by New Livestream. Unable to compete with cable television, which has a more profitable economic model because of its ownership of rights to premium content, the platform sought to serve the middle and lower-end markets of event television. Haot claimed in the interview cited above that New Livestream differentiates itself from competitors like Brightcove and Ooyala in that it aims to be a destination platform, not only providing the technology that makes possible the live-streaming of events, but also the promotion of these events (TechCrunch 2011).

Throughout the *TechCrunch* video interview, Haot persistently described Livestream as a service that could "extend physical events."[30] With the emphasis shifting to the streaming of live events, presencing the viewer became a central value perpetuated through the metatext—an idea perhaps best captured by the new "BE THERE" slogan. Haot claimed that New Livestream provides a "unique" experience of liveness. Such an experience, he insisted, required more than simply allowing the viewer to chat via the platform (he accused the other live-streaming services of doing merely that).

Claims about how the platform sought to redefine live-streaming were made on its new website:

> A live stream is no longer solely about live video. We now support realtime text updates, video clips and photos seamlessly integrated with live video posted from desktop and mobile devices.

It is suggested here that the multiplication of channels and media surrounding and integrated with the event are crucial to the new experience provided by the New Livestream platform. We can point here to similarities with the trend of incorporating social media into the television experience—a topic discussed at greater length in chapter 5, where I consider *The Voice*.

The Volvo Ocean Race's Space of Participation

To capture New Livestream's constellation of liveness, it is worth looking at how the platform featured the Volvo Ocean Race. A tri-annual event, the race in 2011 showcased the New Livestream platform. Because in this particular constellation the metatext and the space of participation are woven together in obvious ways, I consider them here together. In doing so, I discuss both domains in terms of, first, a user relation to liveness (approaching the platform from the viewer's perspective), and then of a producer relation to liveness (from the perspective of someone using the platform to produce channels). In this particular instance, user responses to the platform are notably absent, so they are not considered.

The User Relation to Liveness

With respect to the metatext, discussed in general terms above, I want to briefly point out the two central claims made in the Volvo Ocean Race's promotional texts.[31] These two ideas about the new platform were also visibly implemented on it, giving shape to the space of participation that arose. First, the platform purported to be "social at the core." Second, the platform claimed to be able to bring the viewer "into the race" and to "take [him/her] on the journey out to sea." The promotional video and website equally promoted the idea of a platform providing a *holistic* experience of an event. The slogan "BE THERE" reinforced this claim. As the promotional video for the race summarized many of the platform's new features, it is a fruitful source through which to start delineating the space of participation and to connect it to the two central claims made in the aforementioned metatext.

With respect to its claim of being "social at the core," it can be said that the new platform, compared to the Original Livestream platform, expanded opportunities for social interaction. This widened social dimension is illustrated by two types of relations mediated by the new platform: (1) connections between viewers, and (2) connections between viewers and the event. When it came to connecting viewers to one another, the New Livestream platform, like the Original Livestream, provided viewers with several simple means to interact among themselves. They could share content with others through a chat module and a comments section. In addition, there were several ways for users to interact with the channels featured on the platform: they could comment on (media) posts, follow a channel, "like" posts or share posts via Facebook, Twitter, Tumblr, or email. Furthermore— and here the discontinuity with the old platform is apparent— New Livestream allowed users to create profile pages and have customized homepage feeds where they could receive updates from the channels they followed. They could now follow channels and receive notifications of upcoming events, and, in ways similar to those of social networking sites, choose to follow other users. Moreover, just like on the first Livestream platform, the streamed content had a viewer ticker. However, unlike its predecessor, the new platform expanded this feature by listing on channel pages an event's total number of followers, and how many of these followers were viewing the channel page ("Here Now"). Both features facilitated awareness of other viewers and at the same time made the content appear to have a vast reach and to command mass interest.

As for connecting viewers to the event, the New Livestream platform provided multiple ways for viewers to do so. According to the promotional video, users were offered:

1. An inside view of the event realized by real-time text and photo updates from official photographers integrated with the live video broadcast.
2. Access to photo, text, and video clips sent by the boats through satellite straight to the users on the event-related channels.
3. An instant SMS and email notification directly from the team a user follows as the action unfolds.

These means of connecting to the event correspond to the idea that the new platform was bringing viewers "into the action." The promo went on to boast that a satellite connection facilitated 24/7 updates and "raw access," as the boats were sending media that was made available to viewers in real time. Also, "official" photojournalists on the ground and in the air were said to provide an "inside view" of the action. The video thus perpetuated the values of authenticity and presence, both of which were brought to bear on the liveness of the platform.

In addition to providing viewers with access to the event from multiple perspectives, the new platform also allowed users to receive real-time notifications through email, SMS, or iPhone push notifications. They could also follow the race from the perspective of one of the teams by watching and/or subscribing to a team's Livestream channel. The voiceover in the promo assured viewers that, thanks to all these new features, they would never have to miss any of the action. In short, then, the New Livestream platform was aimed at making viewers feel present at the event by expanding their access to it—both spatially (in terms of the perspective from which one can experience the event) and temporally (in terms of when one can experience it).

But the promo implied that "being there," as a type of experience, also depended on the availability of several technical features of the video stream itself. The first of these was the "adaptive quality selection," which enabled content viewers, based on their connection speeds and computer power, to select their preferred level of video-stream quality. The new platform made it possible to watch up to a 720p HD stream. The second feature mentioned was DVR functionality, which allowed viewers to rewind and replay a video stream. In the stream's top left corner a superimposed graphic identified the content as being either "LIVE" or "DVR." Both of these characteristics suggest that having a "being there" experience at an event is also a matter of not missing out on anything that happens. Having high-definition video and being able to replay moments, it is suggested, helps to facilitate such an experience. These features were also mentioned in a pamphlet, downloadable on the website, that introduced the revamped platform. In this document, stability and scale were presented as core values. More specifically, Livestream boasted that the new platform could stream live to more than one million concurrent viewers. This indicates, once again, its effort to appeal to a more professional client (i.e., producer) base.

The Producer Relation to Liveness

With New Livestream, the company behind it strove for professional production values. On its website, it mentioned three core values for production: quality, speed, and professionalism. To this end it expanded the services it offered. It was now possible to hire production teams from Livestream, and/or to design and customize Facebook apps. Moreover, the company could be consulted about customized campaigns and marketing plans. It had a store where it sold "producer-certified HD encoding solutions and production equipment." In addition to production services and tools, training services in the fields of production and marketing were also offered on the website. Such services were less accessible to individuals, because they required a financial commitment and entailed a resource/skill threshold (including professional tools, time, and know-how).

In June 2012, when the New Livestream platform had just been launched, the service offered only a "producer account." There was no "free" account option, although free accounts continued to be supported through the Original Livestream platform. At this time, several functions such as video embedding, Google Analytics, and APIs were not yet available (although they were introduced later).[32] While the company was developing these features for the new platform, it recommended that users interested in such features sign up for (or continue to use) an Original Livestream premium account.[33] The tools available for producing and stimulating socialization around content, however, expanded significantly compared to the earlier platform. Using the "Web Posting" function, producers could post text, photos, video, or live-video updates on their pages, which operated like blogs. Moreover, there was the option of "Mobile Posting," which was very similar to web posting but done through an iPhone application. The app also enabled the managing of events (creating, deleting, publishing), the creation of event posters, and the monitoring of comments. New Livestream allowed producers to add real-time photos, videos, and text updates before, during, and after an event—anticipating in the process that viewers could "Follow" profiles, "Like" posts, "Comment" on material, and receive "Notifications." Its iPhone app, furthermore, allowed them to post in real time from an iPhone, and the revamped platform also enabled the trimming of video recordings.

What we see is that, over time, Livestream created two rather distinct constellations of liveness for live-streaming. Whereas the first constellation was predicated on turning the user into a kind of television station producer and imitating the practices of live broadcast television, the second constellation emphasized how, for *viewers* specifically, live-streaming could create an experience of being present at an event. It was argued in this context that particular techno-cultural advances had been made that could enhance the immersive experience of the mediated event. At the same time, the new platform targeted a new type of *customer*, interested in distributing "quality" content around events and making that content available and engaging for large audiences. In doing so, it conceptually separated those who used the platform as viewers from those who opted to take on the role of producers.

The Relation between Liveness and Institutionalization

The two constellations discussed in this chapter (the first emerging around Mogulus/Original Livestream, the second associated with New Livestream) shed light on the relation between liveness and institutionalization. I define institutionalization here as a process of "becoming part of a relatively stable cluster of rules, resources and social relations" (Thompson 1995, 12). The connection between liveness and institutionalization comes out of an increasing formalization in the production and distribution of content, i.e., its being subjected to all kinds of standards. The example of Livestream shows that imposing, and respecting, such standards is necessary for liveness to come about. For the users originally targeted by the platform, who were not affiliated with any kind of organization, their inability to deliver content according to these requirements (first, that of continuous, linear programming; later, that of high-quality broadcasting, providing the viewer an experience of "being there") resulted in a failure to deliver liveness as such—whether or not they had even meant to invoke this value in the first place.

Livestream's decision to focus on event television, therefore, can be interpreted as a step toward institutionalization in two connected ways. The first is that they targeted event owners rather than individuals as clients with this programming type. In the Mogulus/Original Livestream constellation, the meaning of the live had still been constructed around the technological infrastructure, and centered on the capacity for live transmission. With the New Livestream platform, the attention shifted to the platform as a site for streaming live events. Here "live" refers to the experience made possible by the platform, functioning as a qualitative category promoting a purportedly superior experience of events. Livestream's shift in orientation, it should be pointed out, runs parallel to the event-TV trend that we see in the broadcast television sector. Although it has been claimed that the contemporary television audience is fragmented (Lotz 2014), people do still watch in large numbers, simultaneously. Jennifer Gillan (2011), for one, has noted how event TV (broadcasts of major sporting events or other special-event programming) continues to attract sizeable audiences. The targeting of event owners by Livestream helped the platform to procure clients with the necessary resources and social relations for producing live experiences.

A second, related reason for interpreting Livestream's decision to focus on event television as a step toward institutionalization lies in its efforts to support formal professionalization. Originally, the Mogulus and Original Livestream rhetoric positioned the platform as a tool for democratizing broadcasting and envisioned bloggers as its users. Unstructured feeds, however, proved too boring to watch, and were unable to draw sufficiently large audiences. With New Livestream, certain textual and aesthetic demands were placed on content, in an attempt to attract more viewers to channels. To support the production of such content, the company started to sell extensive production services and hardware. Institutionalization manifests here in the codes and conventions that are in effect for content production.

In its efforts to stimulate professionalization, the Livestream example also shows how institutionalization is tied up with the paradox that surrounds liveness, briefly discussed at the beginning of this chapter. As Scannell argues, content providers cannot give users direct, unimpeded (and seemingly "natural") access to, and an authentic experience of, a specific event, unless they impose a sufficiently tight structure on it. The demand of linear programming imposed by the Mogulus/Original Livestream platform is a version of this need for structure and control, but New Livestream's shift toward further formalization is even stronger proof of this tendency. In my section on New Livestream, I showed that the greater formalization of the platform meant that the company felt the need to target a new sort of client. At this stage, it no longer aimed to attract bloggers wanting to set up their own "TV stations," but rather hoped to draw event organizers, content owners, celebrities, and artists who were seeking to broadcast their events live. In practice this new orientation meant that henceforward the platform began to target *two sets of audiences*: on the one hand, event owners who needed the platform to produce and distribute content, and on the other, viewers for whom it could function as a destination platform for watching live-streaming content. In stark contrast, the Original Livestream platform targeted users that were eager to assume the joint role of producing and viewing channels.

The platform content's transformation—away from user-generated material and toward more professionally produced offerings—makes manifest the ongoing struggle between the voice of the individual and that of the industry. As Natalie Fenton has found,

> Even accepting that social media engender a form of self-communication that is expressive and creative, self-communication to a mass audience is still the individual trying to be heard above the organization, still the small organization trying to shout louder than the large organization. (2012, 135)

But in the case of Livestream, the individual's voice has ultimately been drowned out. Unable to develop a profitable business model built on user-generated broadcasting akin to television, Livestream paired up with established players who paid for the use of the platform and who, by the same token, were better able to participate in the codes and conventions of "the media."

4

"Live" as an Evaluative Category

In the previous chapter I reflected on Livestream's need to introduce professional standards so as to create television that would be attractive to a large viewership. In this chapter, I set out to explore a case where liveness has failed to take hold, in that the three domains of liveness do not support a single, coherent notion of the live. More specifically, I investigate here the online music-collaboration platform eJamming, made available to the public in a beta version in 2007, and its constellation of liveness as it was constituted during my one-month trial of the platform in April 2011.

My choice of case, here, is influenced first and foremost by eJamming's explicit promotion of itself as "live," in contrast to similar platforms like NINJAM and JackTrip. But also interesting for my purposes is the way that the platform's technology destabilizes the constellation as a whole, thus making more visible the domains of liveness, as well as their actors. In other words, eJamming highlights that liveness is a construction, born out of the combination of players and actions that manifest themselves within the three domains of liveness that I identified in this book's introduction. Here, I reflect what happens in the "black box" of liveness—i.e., in its concealed inner workings—when it is opened through the platform's failure to deliver on user expectations of liveness. This not only reveals the central role of technology in the construction, inviting a comparison between the concepts of real time and liveness, but also discloses liveness as an evaluative category.

The eJamming Metatext: Empowering Musicians

To delineate the platform's metatext, I examine the eJamming website as well as promotional materials that can be accessed through the site. Unlike other online music-collaboration platforms, eJamming is explicitly promoted as being "live" throughout its metatext. The reiteration of the term makes "liveness" its overarching promise. The associations raised by the platform through its metatext, in combination with its technological infrastructure and user responses, contribute to the meaning and value of liveness in its constellation.

The home page of the eJamming website as it looked in the summer of 2011 was styled like an amplifier stack, with six musicians playing instruments layered over it (see figure 3). The term "live" was featured in three separate taglines. The first, beneath the eJamming logo, read: "Now play and record together live with musicians anywhere in the world." The second, figured below a simulated control panel on the bottom left that featured the buttons "Play," "Record," and "Rehearse," read "Together Live Online," a slogan styled as a stamp. Finally, the catchphrase "Jam live with musicians anywhere in the world" appeared below a green "Sign up" button. The promise of liveness, reiterated throughout the website as an experience the platform could deliver, acquired meaning in relation to notions of real time and sociality.

The term "real time" was featured far less prominently in the metatext than the term "live." An embedded video on the website carried the introductory text "Watch and Listen as 3 Musicians Play Live Over the Internet in Real Time," thus providing a first clue that the platform's producers regarded the concepts not as interchangeable but as meaning different things. In addition, the term was used in a page header that read: "eJamming AUDiiO—The Collaborative Network for Musicians Creating Together Online in Real Time." The facilitation of playing together in real time, moreover, is one

Fig. 3:   A snapshot of the eJamming home page (on July 10, 2011, via the Wayback Machine)

of the first points eJamming addressed in its mission statement. Later in this chapter, I further reflect on the site's promises and its relation to liveness when dealing with its space of participation and its user responses.

The terms "connectivity" and "collaboration," which were used recurrently in the metatext, relate to the other main theme, namely sociality. This is also evident from a promotional video on the website that explained how eJamming worked. Here, the platform was explicitly aligned with other social networks:

> All the things you would normally expect to find in any social network are available here except we are specific to live music jamming.

In addition, connectivity was highlighted through the platform design, specifically in the mini-profiles and the embedded chat window featured on the site. The site's "Learn More" section addressed the promise of sociality as well:

Check out who's in the eJamming Lobby. Look over their instruments and musical influences in their mini-profile. Chat with them.
Then invite them to a Session. Or join theirs.
You can talk live. Decide what to play.
Then jam together. Live. Online.

This run-through of how eJamming works draws on a familiar narrative: a person walks into a bar, looks around, spots a match, initiates a round of small talk, and finally, in this particular instance, ends up making music with others. The metaphor depicts the platform as casual and accessible. It also draws an analogy between the platform and a building lobby, suggesting that people are coming, going, and waiting around. In short, eJamming is characterized as a place to meet new people. This particular platform concept was also underscored in the website's mission statement, where it was characterized as a "central meeting ground." The subscription store contained a text that read: "It's easy to subscribe to *connect to a world of musicians* on eJamming ® AUDiiO" (my emphasis). And so, in the metatext, the platform was repeatedly framed as a social space.

But aside from being social in the sense of bringing musicians into contact with one another, eJamming was also portrayed as a site for collaboration. This is most explicit, of course, in the way it labeled itself as an online music-collaboration platform. The repetition of the word "together" in the "Learn More" section supported such an assessment as well:

With eJamming, you can be a beginner who just wants to connect with other musicians.
To jam. Sing and harmonize together.
Rehearse together. Create together. Even learn some new techniques.
Or just hang out together.
Even when your jam mates are 8000 miles apart.

In addition to portraying the platform as an easy way to connect with a vast community of musicians scattered across the globe, the platform highlighted sociality in another way. For instance, in October 2010, eJamming had three musicians play for a club full of residents in Linden Lab's 3D Virtual

World *Second Life*. This showcase calls attention to eJamming's desire to connect musicians and their fans through live performances (for, indeed, the event was promoted as "live").

By drawing on liveness, the particular relationship between real time and the social, eJamming promoted itself as a tool for empowering musicians. This argument was found most prominently in the platform's vision of how it would "enable" users. More specifically, the platform argued that it empowered musicians in three ways, outlined below. Those different forms of empowerment were directly tied in with the website and platform's tendency to adopt a garage-band look and feel, and together defined the "liveness" of the platform.

The first form of empowerment concerned the way that eJamming can bring together a geographically dispersed group of musicians. The barriers of physical geography, it was implied at the time, could be overcome by the togetherness and sense of connection facilitated by the service among its users: "Across town. Across the country. Or if you want to, even across the ocean." The metatext invoked geographic locations to further underscore this point. In the *Second Life* experiment just discussed, the band's geographical configuration was emphasized in promotional materials. Similarly, on the home page of the eJamming website captured in figure 3, two of the text bubbles accompanying the six musicians portrayed gave a geographical reference. In YouTube videos that showcased eJamming sessions, finally, the cities of the participants were a central part of the explanation of how the platform worked. This form of empowerment was considered to have two advantages. First, users could take part "right from [their] home" and, second, they didn't have to haul their instruments and equipment somewhere else.

The second form of empowerment centered on time rather than space. As the eJamming website put it:

> In today's busy world, the hardest thing is to find time to make music. . . . You can even make new friends. So you can play together. . . . Live. Right from home. Whenever you want.

This snippet of text captures a point mentioned not only on the website but also repeatedly in promotional talks and materials. People can make music together whenever they want, since at any time there would be an opportunity to find others to jam with. The availability of band members or other musicians to play with would no longer be an issue.

A third form of empowerment was highlighted in eJamming's mission statement. Here, the platform was presented as a space for music students to connect with their teachers. But unlike the other two forms of empowerment, this educational use was put forth only in the "About Us" section on the eJamming website.

The Space of Participation

The eJamming metatext, as I have demonstrated, promotes the empowerment of musicians by drawing on notions of real time and sociality. In analyzing the space of participation for the platform, I want to consider how techno-cultural, economic, and legal forces shape user participation. Although these forces overlap and interrelate, I discuss them separately for the sake of clarity.

In terms of techno-cultural forces, it is important to note that eJamming necessitates several basic requirements, most fundamentally access to a computer and an internet connection. A Windows or Mac OS X operating system is necessary for the computer to install and run the software (the open-source Linux operating system is not supported). And, of course, a musical instrument and (built-in) microphone are needed.

One of eJamming's technological advantages over its competitors is its software's compatibility with both Musical Instrument Digital Interface (MIDI) instruments (which many conventional instruments have been converted to) and non-MIDI instruments (such as drums, violins and other string instruments, and voice). Nevertheless, to counter latency, the company strongly recommends the use of an external audio interface to plug in instruments. By directly plugging an instrument into the soundcard, or by using the internal microphone, for instance, the user of a Mac computer would create a 40 msec delay—a circumstance that, as I elaborate, proved very problematic to musicians.[34]

A broadband connection was not sufficient in itself for the service to function properly. For two musicians to join a session and make stable use of the platform, a minimum upload speed of 400 kbps was required. To use the platform at its full capacity—having four musicians play together in real time—each user would have to have an upload speed of 800 kbps. In the previous chapter, I noted that the average upload speed in the United States was 595 kbps in 2010, so, as with Livestream, we should ask how many people actually had the proper resources to use the eJamming platform to its full potential.

Reliance on broadband connectivity brings forward what is perhaps *the* biggest challenge to online music-collaboration tools: latency. Latency refers to delays in network processing resulting from technological variables such as bandwidth. Because physical wires transport the bits of a data stream, distance is another variable that can cause latency (Davis 2008). Indeed, eJamming performs more optimally when connecting peers are geographically closer to one another.[35] In an article on the effects of network delay on musical performance, Driessen et al. observe:

> To achieve a good user experience the latency over the network has to be within reasonable bounds. If the delay is excessive, then the musicians will not be able to maintain a consistent tempo. (2011, 76–7)

Renaud et al. (2007) have researched ensemble performance threshold (EPT), the maximum level of delay that would still allow musicians to play in synchronization. In their experience, this is 25 msec or less, end to end (from source to destination).[36]

Typically, online music-collaboration platforms encounter the following types of latency: sound hardware latency (>5 msec), perceptual CODEC latency (>20 msec), and network latency (>40 msec).[37] This makes it difficult, if not impossible, for eJamming to attain its goal of real-time synchronization. The latency between two players on eJamming in jam mode, as registered by a user in 2010, was 60 msec, significantly higher than the EPT considered ideal for musicians.[38]

The problem of latency is not unique to scenarios mediated by an online platform. All musical experience is subject to a lag between the time of production and that of consumption (Auslander 2008; Kobrin 2007). Even an orchestra is no exception:

> In an orchestra, there is a roughly 1 millisecond-per-foot delay between, say, a flautist and a bassist, who can be seated up to 50 feet apart. Humans typically notice delays of 15 to 60 milliseconds, depending on the individual. That's one reason an orchestra needs a conductor to keep players in sync. (Kobrin 2007, n.p.)

But while latency is not unique to technological mediation, the multiplication of forms of mediation in online music collaboration—introduced through hardware, software, and along networks—adds to the latency incurred. This, paired with EPT, makes latency a central problem for these platforms.

To date, online music-collaboration platforms have found it extremely challenging to facilitate EPT. They have dealt with latency differently, each introducing a series of "fixes" to the problem. Novel Intervallic Network Jamming Architecture for Music (NINJAM) has found that collaboration unhampered by latency can be achieved only by *increasing* the delay in sent audio by one measure (one bar) and having musicians synchronize to music generated in the previous measure. As explained on the NINJAM website:

> Since the inherent latency of the Internet prevents true real-time synchronization of the jam, and playing with latency is weird (and often uncomfortable), NINJAM provides a solution by making latency (and the weirdness) much longer.[39]

Simply put, the service has chosen to incorporate latency into the experience, rather than attempt to eliminate it. For this reason NINJAM has been said to offer "fake-time" (Renaud, Carôt, and Rebelo 2007) and "near-real-time" (Van Buskirk 2007). These labels, used to describe NINJAM's strategy, help to establish the definition of real time as something realized only when technology is pushed to achieve "absolute" simultaneity.

The eJamming AUDiiO software, in contrast, initially adopted a combination of approaches to minimize latency on different fronts (Greene 2007). First, it decreased file sizes sent over the network with (de)compression algorithms. Second, rather than sending audio streams through a remote server, it connected the online musicians peer to peer.[40] Third, the audio of the individual users was time-stamped to the millisecond of production, and the clocks on users' computers were synchronized to that of the user who initiated the session. This allowed for the music to be synchronized at a slightly delayed moment.

Later, in 2011, the eJamming website made several suggestions to help users themselves reduce their experience of latency. For instance, because the platform works via peer-to-peer connections, all users needed to configure their routers and open the "IN" and "OUT" ports. It was also suggested that users connect to the router via an Ethernet cable rather than through a wireless connection, and that they should limit the data usage of others connected to their router. Moreover, eJamming recommended that users wear headphones during sessions, so that they could focus on the overall music being produced rather than the sound coming from an individual instrument. Finally, as an additional measure to reduce latency, Windows users were advised to download and install Audio Stream Input/Output software to allow for a direct audio path to the sound card/audio interface.

Aside from latency issues, the platform's graphical user interface (GUI) also shaped how musicians used and experienced eJamming—what it afforded and what it constrained. During my trial period, eJamming offered two distinct modes of online music collaboration: "Jam mode," a form of virtual rehearsing, and "Overdub mode," as if one were playing in some kind of virtual recording studio. In "Jam mode," a maximum of four geographically dispersed musicians could create music together over the internet in sync. However, in contrast to "Overdub mode," this setting did not allow for the recording of the sessions.

In "Overdub mode," eJamming enabled long-distance recording collaborations through a "Virtual Recording Studio" (VRS). This, of course, was also a way of circumventing latency. Here, a musician could lay down a track with limited latency, and then previously recorded tracks were placed on top of it (users could record up to sixteen MIDI and sixteen audio tracks). Session participants could listen to the tracks and converse with one another about them. The 3.0 software version allowed only the musicians taking part in a session to listen to what was being performed. In late 2010, eJamming announced on its website that it would soon release JamCastLive, which would allow sessions to be broadcast over the internet. In a 2015 interview with *Guitarcoach Magazine* a representative of eJamming claimed that they were almost done developing JamCastle, which would facilitate the streaming of performances live to smartphones (Cianci 2015).

Unlike Facebook, Pinterest, or Instagram, eJamming is based on a shared interest in music-making. The platform is branded in its metatext as a space for music collaboration, as the website makes clear through text (e.g., its slogan) and image (e.g., the garage band theme). However, it has provided several social functions. Upon setting up an account, users create a profile (having the option of providing basic information, both personal and music-related), are able to search for and find other musicians, and can create a network of contacts by "friending" others. The profile fields prompted users to define their "musical influences" and "talents," in addition to allowing them to upload and store music files for sharing with others. Moreover, an internal messaging system allowed them to send (asynchronous) messages to other members. Also, the home page, referred to as the "Lobby," included a chat box. All these features were meant to support online jamming.

The eJamming forum provided a space where questions of social etiquette played out. In 2011 I encountered a prime example of this sort of dialogue among users. Because eJamming users were unable to netcast sessions (i.e., broadcast them over the internet), people began to ask whether it was acceptable practice to simply join a session but not play; the answer was "no."[41] So, although purely technically speaking, users could join sessions but remain "lurkers," this practice was emphatically discouraged through social condemnation. Here, we clearly see a cultural constraint take effect.

In addition to techno-cultural currents shaping the space of participation, economic forces affect interaction and participation on eJamming. It should first be repeated that eJamming has a very different business model than the other three cases explored in this book: for starters, all users have to pay a subscription fee (so in this respect, it resembles the New Livestream but not Mogulus/Original Livestream). This is important to note, as different tradeoffs occur when consumers are paying for a particular service or product, and they tend to feel more entitled to criticize and demand improvements when not satisfied.

So, in addition to having access to a computer and an internet connection, to use eJamming people also need to purchase a subscription plan (in 2011, $9.95 a month, $24.95 for three months, or $89.95 a year). While computers and internet access are common in most Western countries, the subscription plan could prove a constraint (cf. Needleman 2007), particularly for those wishing to use the platform for band practice. For a four-member band, for example, paying at least $360 a year collectively to use the service is decidedly more expensive than playing together with friends in someone's garage.

Finally, legal forces shape user interaction and participation on eJamming. Before installing the software, users have to agree to its terms and conditions of use. By doing so, they bind themselves to a set of rules and obligations. These regulations went as far as addressing the issue of online identity:

> You may not impersonate or misrepresent yourself as another person (including celebrities), another eJamming user, an eJamming, Inc employee, or a civic or government leader; eJamming, Inc reserves the right to reject or block any eJamming service user name which could be deemed to be an impersonation or misrepresentation of your identity, or a misappropriation of another person's name or identity.

And as in the case of Livestream, copyright issues play a particularly important role in how the platform and participation on it are organized. At the time of consultation, the user agreement for eJamming stated that users had to pay license fees to publicly perform and/or mechanically reproduce any copyrighted materials. In a session with others, users jointly acquired ("by virtue of their interaction") the copyright for what they had collaboratively created in the session.⁴² However, by agreeing to eJamming's terms, users granted the platform the right to freely use (reproduce, modify, adapt, and/or publish) content to promote the platform.

With regard to performances of non-original material, eJamming claimed to be negotiating so-called blanket licenses from the organizations holding music-performance rights to allow registered users to perform these songs and other compositions. In 2015, in their terms and conditions, they stated that they were still negotiating these licenses. Such legal issues are relevant to the constellation of liveness in that they may have contributed to a delay in the introduction of netcasting on the platform.

Reviewing the space of participation, one sees how users can interact and participate on the platform, enabling a better understanding of what the platform affords and constrains. In light of the promises made through eJamming's metatext about the real-time encounters with others supposedly mediated by the platform, a conflict immediately surfaces. After all, real technological challenges stand in the way of such promises actually being delivered. I return to this point shortly, as these challenges do, indeed, make it difficult to realize liveness.

User Responses: Liveness as Value

What a platform's users say about it can tell us what meanings they attribute to its liveness. Therefore, it is useful to take stock of the threads (both permanent and user-initiated), posts, and views expressed on the eJamming forum, and to reflect on the topics addressed there.⁴³ Equally interesting are comments posted outside the eJamming platform; I therefore discuss comments found through Google searching; these views, however, are of a different nature and address different topics from those expressed on the eJamming forum. They are less concerned with solving specific technical problems— probably because the eJamming forum provided a direct connection to eJamming staff and other users—and more directed toward sharing general experiences and opinions about the platform. The user responses I focus on from these sources are those that were most likely directed at the 2011 software release (eJamming AUDiiO 3.0). My aim is not to disclose the ideas of a representative sample of users but rather to zoom in on those comments and practices that reflect on the liveness of the platform. Overall, most of the people making these comments were dissatisfied with the platform and found eJamming to be more suitable for casual than professional use.

Having surveyed all these sources in 2011, as well as activity on the platform more broadly, I can infer that user discontent concerned topics that were also the main themes of the metatext: real time and sociality. With regard to real-time experience, users were frustrated that they could not play fully synchronized sessions. As for sociality, users expected both the existence of an active community of musicians and the ability to share sessions with an audience over the internet. The interrelation between real time and sociality is what the platform draws on to promote its "live" experience; therefore, claims regarding these topics can be read as reflections on the kind of liveness promised by the platform.

Real Time

Nothing posted on the eJamming forum in 2011 indicated that users were having problems with real-time connectivity. But when I returned to the forum in 2015, there were threads on latency issues and tips to deal with the problem. On other forums it was always a dominant topic, and users explicitly articulated their frustration with the platform. It is worth looking more closely at a few sample posts to flesh out the discontent vented in these contributions, and to identify the problems experienced by eJamming's users.

User Learjeff, for instance, made the following comment:

> But they [eJamming] say, 'The whole point is to focus on the music that one hears, as opposed to on the sounds coming directly from one's instrument'. Bad idea: we need to relearn how to play, to have good timing with a delayed monitor. Sounds like something a non-musician would say![44]

In that same thread, JohnnySixString mentioned that the service does not work for counting off or for playing covers, but works "pretty well" for "improv and stuff"—even if he was coming in a measure behind others.[45]

The founders of eJamming, Gail Kantor and Alan Glueckman, had responded to concerns about latency in a 2007 interview at Indie-Music.com:

> But after playing over eJamming for a while, we've found that musicians can play ahead of the beat even with delays of 120 milliseconds, and vocalists have been able to adjust even to 60 milliseconds. The best way to work with eJamming is to listen over headphones, and focus on what you're hearing, and not what your hands or voice are doing, and performing to the synchronized audio in your headphones. (Glass 2007, n.p.)

The quotation reflects the situation in 2007, when eJamming was still beta (and thus free to use). The numerous comments in the years that followed, after it had been turned into a paid service, indicate that the problem still lingered. Rob is just one of the users who complained about latency in 2011:

> As a paying eJamming customer, I play online from SF, CA to St Louis, MO, and yes lag is about 50ms. So no, it doesn't sound great playing a song. You'll never feel locked in. However, it can still be fun for casual use, but the software is very buggy. . . . They seemed [*sic*] to have stopped all development work on it now. I mean how can they sustain development if there are only 10 people in the lobby at all times.[46]

Rob's experience is in line with that of JohnnySixString. Both find that eJamming AUDiiO can be fun to use for improvisational jamming sessions, but that for the playing of actual songs, latency is a real obstacle. Interestingly, then, the connotation attached to the platform's name—one of playful improvisation—did not prevent it from being criticized for not enabling users to play together "properly." So, while the metatext raised the expectation that users would be able to make music together on the "live" platform, actual users complained that it failed to deliver on these promises. In so doing, they disclosed what they expected of the platform.

Sociality

But Rob's post, mentioning how there are only "10 people in the lobby at all times," also highlights that the dissatisfaction with eJamming went beyond its failure to technologically mediate a jam session without the nuisance of latency. Here emerges another strand of criticism, this time connected to the issue of sociality. From the online comments and the use of the eJamming forum, I gather that eJamming was also unable to realize the social end of the live promise for its users, and for two main reasons: because users felt there was a lack of other musicians to jam with, and because they were unable to perform for an audience.

Homing in on these issues in a post on the Music Player Network forum, JohnnySixString complained that the platform was too sparsely populated:

> Every time I have ever tried the eJamming 30 day trial, over the past couple of years now, there simply aren't enough people using it. Unless you and some friends plan to log on at the same time to play, there needs to be a butt load more people in the pool in order to find someone else to play with. . . . There never seems to be more than 20 people on at once and that seems to be at peak.[47]

However, he also expressed hope that the company's intention of partnering with Fender would boast public awareness of eJamming and increase the number of registered users. Nevertheless, even after the Fender partnership began in March 2011, users still found themselves having to schedule jam sessions with people they already knew or had solicited on the forum, for want of a large community of musicians in the site's Lobby.

A 2010 comment by armystrongamerican on the YouTube video *ONLINESESSIONSSUCK* (2009) similarly read:

> i play the drums…this site sucks for that, everytime i went in the room there was no one there! come on! how am i supposed to play when everyone is freakin gone! and the only people that do show up is jamming [the platform's founder] who is a complete dick or his wife! wtf man this site is a joke!

i would never pay money just to sit in a fuckin room and
day dream!

As evident from the profanity in the concluding sentences,
users could get extremely irritated that eJamming consistently
failed to deliver an active pool of musicians to potentially
play with. My own experience with the platform confirms
the substance of this complaint: I never found more than
three ongoing sessions or more than seven people online at
the site.[48]

The relative popularity of the topic "JAM" on the eJamming forum also underscores the sense that there were usually
few musicians online to jam with. This thread was set up to
help users schedule sessions with one another. Equally revealing is that about one-third of the requests for extra features
on the eJamming forum concerned the addition of social
functions, for example Buddy Lists, Messaging, or a JAM
Schedule. These functions could be used for appeals to make
appointments to jam.

However, not having others to jam with was just one of
the users' concerns with regard to the sociality afforded by
the platform. Another was its inability to facilitate the sharing
of active sessions with an audience. This was a central issue
in several online forums. On the eJamming forum, Ben
Brannan made the following remark in a request for a "listen
in" feature:

> This is exactly what I'd love to sdd [*sic*]. I signed up hoping
> to put on virtual concerts with friends. So I thought there'd
> be some sort of listen URL stream. I think this would seriously
> boost the amount of people interested in ejamming if this
> feature were enabled.[49]

In the forum's "Help" section, some users asked how to
enable listening in. eJamming responded to users' requests on
its homepage's FAQ section, where it promised to offer netcasting sometime in the foreseeable future. Perhaps this can
be seen as a form of consensus among users and facilitators
as to what should be part of the software's functionality in
order to make eJamming live up to its promises.

In the absence of an official platform feature to enable the
sharing of sessions with an audience, a dedicated eJamming

user named Cartman initiated the RaDiiO project, which ran intermittently from 2009 to 2010. The birth of the project, it can be argued, also attests to the users' expectation that they should—and would—be able to share sessions with an audience. Cartman modified the platform to enable sessions to be netcast, seeking to create an internet band with musicians from around the world and to broadcast live sessions over the internet in real time.

In the blog he kept about the project, Cartman reflected on some of his other problems using the platform. His criticisms echo the central topics I have identified in the eJamming metatext. For instance, he mentioned the consistent shortage of active users on the platform, which he attributed to the lack of "a focal point to sustain people's interest and engender a sense of community." Sociality on the platform, as Cartman observes, can be engendered only if it can generate sufficient interest among users, so that they in turn can contribute and augment its social dimension and scale.

Cartman also wrote on the experience of latency, which, he found, increased as more users joined a session; this is important with respect to the complaints surrounding real time mentioned earlier. On his blog, he stated that latency problems required him to make artistic compromises during sessions: the group he played with, for example, chose songs they thought would be least affected by delays.

The RaDiiO project was temporarily suspended in late 2009, in anticipation of a new software release for eJamming. However, by April 2010, a listen-in feature had still not been realized, and the show was briefly revived. But the relations between the group of enthusiasts propelling the project and eJamming had, according to the blog, gone from bad to worse. Following additional setbacks, one of the project's regular volunteers dropped out, and the shows were abandoned for good. Although eJamming refused to participate in the project because it sought to protect its established business, both its mission statement and its 2010 *Second Life* marketing stunt strongly suggest that the company, like eJamming's users, was convinced that because it was offering a platform for live jamming, it needed to facilitate the sharing of online performances with an audience.

User responses to eJamming, as we have seen, show that the platform has met with a fair amount of criticism. In considering the platform's failure to deliver on its promise of liveness, I have also shown here how in situations like these the three domains of liveness come to the fore, as such failure is revealed precisely by the clashes between these domains. In the process, liveness presents itself as an evaluative category.

In users' reactions to eJamming, they referenced ideas that they believed were promoted through the notion of liveness proposed by the metatext. The experience of the platform, in other words, was being assessed *through* the category of the "live." In eJamming's attempt to position itself as a go-to platform for online music collaboration, it employs liveness to promote value. In this way, the constellation of liveness could also bring to the surface the particular shortcomings of the platform. Remarkably, other music-collaboration platforms face a lack of available participants at any given time, too—but because eJamming claimed to be live, its failure to deliver made users feel that certain promises of liveness had not been met.

The "live," in a way, functions as placeholder for the set of promises made by the platform. The metatext, indeed, frames how the liveness of a platform is to be understood. Meanwhile, the same technological basis, through its interaction with the metatext and user responses, can establish a range of values for the "live" experience. This is most evident in traditional television. Although its space of participation is fairly consistent across programs, particularly prior to the advent of transmedia formats and social TV, different values were attributed to the "live," each drawing on a particular relation between real-time connectivity and sociality. Whereas a sporting event, for instance, might emphasize presence, a news program might seek instead to highlight the authenticity of its reporting, and a scripted series might broadcast an episode live primarily to play on the excitement that anything could go wrong.

The failure of eJamming to deliver on expectations about the platform's liveness helps me introduce what I call "tensions surrounding the live"—the particular conflicts that emerge over the meaning and promise of the live. With eJamming, however, these tensions are so prominent that a complete debilitation of liveness has occurred as liveness has failed to be realized. In chapters 5 and 6, I explore those tensions further using other case studies. This will help me, in turn, to compare mediation in the broadcast media era and the social media era.

Between Liveness and Real Time

Analyzing the eJamming metatext also revealed that liveness and real time were not positioned as interchangeable experiences (consider, for instance, the remark on the website that musicians "played live in real time"). However, in discussing the technological forces shaping its space of participation, I demonstrated that real time is *part* of what enabled eJamming to make a claim to liveness. In the user responses, latency problems prevented musicians from experiencing the platform as "live." Here the close kinship between real time and liveness also presents itself, albeit in a different way. Taken together, these claims and reactions indicate that the term "real time" references a technological capacity. Even though what is considered real time is context-dependent, it is temporally quantifiable (i.e., quantifiable in terms of speed), as opposed to liveness, which isn't. Think, for example, of features like real-time stock trading and the surveillance camera, which are void of any claim to sociality and therefore, I would argue, to liveness. So while real time is certainly an axis of liveness, liveness exceeds this technological capacity, and can be provided only in combination with a position on the axis of sociality.

The question as to why many other online music-collaboration platforms have not been promoted as live is still on the table. Based on the previous chapter, I would propose that this relates to these other platforms being open-source, as opposed to commercial, projects. Open-source platforms promote collaboration, whereas commercial platforms are profit-oriented, working within an institutional sphere. Thus, they have a vested interest in employing liveness to promote value.

5
Social TV and the Multiplicity of the Live

The introduction to this book drew attention to the multiple forms of the live in the social media era. In this chapter, I delve further into the question of the multiplicity of the live by studying social TV. In doing so, I position the phenomenon called "social TV" within a lineage of post-television strategies centered on participation and critically engage claims in popular discourse regarding its sociality.

As the latest configuration of television, social TV can be understood as a strategy seeking to bring back audiences to the schedules of network broadcasters. The format transforms the viewer into a "viewser" (Harries 2004), as it provides audiences the opportunity not only to view but also to participate in and around the program. Specifically, I examine NBC television's popular reality-singing competition *The Voice* (2011–), primarily its first season, focusing on the constellation of liveness in its live shows.[50] These types of live shows, common to reality competitions in general, are established as media events in that they are live, pre-planned, and seek to captivate a large audience (Puijk 2010).

The Voice has positioned itself as the pinnacle of social TV, which is one of the reasons I chose to look closely at it. Studying *The Voice* paves the way for pinpointing some of the conditions in which liveness comes into effect, because in the constellation of its live shows, numerous live constructs interact with one another to inform the three domains I have been examining in this book—metatext, space of participation, and user responses.

Having developed my take on liveness in the previous chapters, where I homed in on institutionalization and the constructedness of liveness, respectively, I now switch gears, using liveness as a tool to analyze the relationship between broadcast media and social media. Here I first delineate the constellation of liveness for *The Voice*'s live shows, then consider the tensions that emerged between the three domains of the live. The choice of examining the American adaptation of the show (it was copied from what was originally a Dutch program) is important here. The United States comprises multiple time zones and, as it happens, the show's practice of tape delay highlights a key issue for this chapter: the disconnect between the schedules of broadcasters and those of its "empowered" viewers. In addition, the show's gradual "tweaking" of its social media strategy over the course of several seasons, which essentially altered the meaning of the live for the live shows, also points to another tension, one that pertains to audience participation.

Social TV: A Strategy of Broadcast TV

Television has always been characterized as a flexible medium (Uricchio 2009) marked by "hybridity" (Bennett 2011; Jacobs 2000). Recently, with new sites for production and reception, it has even become impossible to speak of television in the singular (Lotz 2014; Turner and Tay 2009), because the medium is now highly diversified. Social TV is one of the more recent televisual configurations—and one that has attracted widespread attention in popular discourse.[51]

In her book *The Television Will Be Revolutionized* (2014), Amanda Lotz explores the characteristics of three main phases of American television history, which she identifies as the network era (approximately 1952 to the mid-1980s), the multi-channel transition (mid-1980s to mid-2000s), and the post-network era (mid-2000s to the present).[52] The network era was typified by limited program choice, a linear viewing experience, and appointment television. It was then that "the medium [television] gained its status as a primary cultural institution because network-era programming could and did reach such vast audiences" (Lotz 2014, 34).

Because people were watching the same shows, and at the same time, television became known as a topical resource for discussion, prompting what is commonly referred to as "water-cooler conversation." Starting in the 1980s, the multi-channel transition introduced more viewer choice, thanks to distribution systems such as cable and satellite, as well as greater viewer control, through devices like the remote control and videocassette recorders. Then, in the post-network era, audience fragmentation intensified with the advent of digital technologies that increased the number of available channels and degree of viewer control. These changes led to the further erosion of network control over how and when viewers watched certain programs. Television from then on has been seen as less "social," purportedly incapable of prompting water-cooler conversation. Whereas forty to fifty percent of television households in the United States watched popular shows in the network era (Lotz 2014, 47), in 2015 viewership of *The Big Bang Theory*, the second-ranked regularly sched-uled program in primetime that year, attracted around eigh-teen percent of U.S. TV households.[53]

These last observations helped form the popular narrative in which "social TV" (Dumenco 2011) as a strategy is situ-ated. This is a narrative that can be broken down into three parts:

1. the television audience has dispersed,
2. but by embracing the real time of social media platforms as an opportunity, the lost sociality of television can be rekindled,
3. and when television networks have done so, the ratings of its programs have increased.

The descriptor "social TV" is somewhat confusing, as it suggests that sociality is new to broadcast television—which of course it is not. In the postwar United States, televi-sions at bars were a source of amusement and conversation (McCarthy 2001), a tradition that persists in today's (sports) bars. In the 1980s, there was experimentation with audience members messaging through the TV screen (Jonietz 2010); online forums for discussing television shows emerged in the early years of the internet (Baym 2000). Each of these particular television configurations emphasized different forms of social interaction.

Aside from its overarching assumption that people are very eager for a "participatory" form of television viewing, other aspects of the narrative explaining social TV are problematic as well. First off, while today's popular television series attract substantially fewer viewers than those in the network era, Super Bowl XLIX in 2015 set a U.S. television record, drawing 114.4 million viewers (49.7 percent of American television households) and thus became "the most-watched show in U.S. television history" (Taibi 2015). In fact, live-event television is expected to continue to provide a market for broadcasting because such programming reliably attracts large audiences (Turner 2009). The conclusion that mass audiences are a thing of the past, in any case, overlooks the sizeable audiences that particular television genres continue to attract.

Another questionable presupposition behind the common narrative about television focuses on the idea of the water-cooler conversation. Television has indeed always been social, but we need to be careful not to fixate on continuities with earlier forms of practice—to the exclusion of significant changes. In social TV, I would suggest, important differences have emerged as a result of, for instance, the technological specificities of Twitter (e.g., its 140-character limit), which change the way communication takes place—but also because in the real-time of Twitter the "conversation" happens during, rather than after, the event.

What's more, the leaders of networks and cable channels celebrate how social media platforms are employed to combat audience fragmentation and to stimulate viewers to return to appointment-TV watching (Highfield, Harrington, and Bruns 2013; Slutsky and Patel 2011). They see platform proliferation and the harnessing of audience participation as a low-cost, strategic effort to retain and build audiences (Steinberg 2009b; Ytreberg 2009). Several social TV experiments have been ratings success stories, but other efforts have disappointed: viewership for the 2011 Academy Awards, while making heavy use of social media during the program, was nine percent lower than the previous year's broadcast (Guthrie 2011). Reductive, causal relations drawn between social media use in television and higher ratings simply does not bear scrutiny: the suggestion that the expansion of TV shows into the social media realm would alone result in higher ratings overlooks the many other factors that determine a program's success.

As a strategy, social TV demonstrates the television industry's continued investment in what Jenkins et al. (2013) call an "appointment-based model" of watching television. Such a model is of interest to the industry, they claim, because revenue generated through advertisements from first-run content is the most significant source of income for television studios and networks.

Relations between Social Media and Television

Having considered social TV as a strategic response to audience fragmentation, I now move on to examining the relation between social media and television in practice. Analyzing how television shows make use of social media brings forward four different types of relationships with the program text: extension, overlay, enveloping, and integration. The four uses of social media that I identify below can complement and interact with one another in different configurations. I discuss each, giving examples for clarification that center on entertainment programs, though they can also be found in other television genres.[54]

Extensions

The first relation concerns the use of social media as an extension of television programming (Ytreberg 2009; Gillan 2011), coinciding with what Jenkins (2006) has called "transmedia storytelling." Jenkins defines this term as the practice of extending storylines and developing characters across multiple media channels (e.g., games, films, books, websites, and webisodes). Here, audiences are asked to seek out information across multiple platforms and to make connections among the content they encounter there. Each platform offers a unique entry point to the franchise.

As extensions, social media platforms serve the purpose of facilitating an ongoing relation between the audience and the format. They extend the lived relationship beyond the experience of initial consumption (Caldwell 2000). A show's official website, for instance, offers viewers several ways of entering a show's narrative, linking to various types of related content. Today's shows' hosts and producers are active on social media platforms, too, creating yet more new entry points to the experience of the show. Here, television functions as a medium that combines broadcasting with narrowcast forms of address on digital platforms (Beyer et al. 2007; Castells 2009; Gillan 2011).

Overlays

The second relation between social media and telecasts is one I propose to call "overlay." It is an aesthetic relation, and similar to what has been conceptualized as "hypermediacy" (Bolter and Grusin 2000) in that it concerns the multiplication of media. In using "overlay," however, I specifically target the incorporation of other media in television.

In the United States in 2009, Fox television aired what turned out to be a controversial "tweet-peat" experiment involving repeats of its shows *Fringe* and *Glee*. This experiment illustrates well what overlay is, and also points to one of its pitfalls. It was intended as a Q&A between fans and the shows' cast members and producers, as well as a place for episode commentary. Tweets scrolled across the bottom third of the screen—which prompted viewer complaints that the overlay had blocked large portions of the onscreen action (see also Steinberg 2009a). Although this would seem a straightforward interaction between Twitter and television, it shows how efforts to embed social media in programming have been, and continue to be, part of a strained process of trial and error. An easy fix to this problem has been the emergence of the second screen (primarily smartphones and tablets), which allows viewsers to interact with and around the content without it interfering with the onscreen action. But less intrusive ways of incorporating tweets have been developed as well.

Enveloping

Yet another way that social media can relate to television programming is through enveloping. Diverse media platforms aggregate a community around a TV program's content and facilitate communication among participating members of the audience. This relation differs from extension because here these platforms are means for users to communicate with one another in real time while watching a program, as opposed to communicating before or after the broadcast. Twitter, in particular, boasts that it lends itself well to this practice.[55] As has been argued, enveloping provides a strong incentive for live viewing (Highfield, Harrington, and Bruns 2013).

Besides Twitter, other platforms also offer(ed) this type of relation, providing a sphere for conversation around the shared text. In 2008, ABC Family started hosting "online viewing parties," and CBS also experimented with social media by introducing "social viewing rooms."[56] Both initiatives provided viewers the opportunity to watch shows together and chat about them in real time on Facebook or on the network's website. In addition, they also posted polls and competitive quizzes as a way of bringing interactive activities to the platform.

In this context, we should also consider the emergence of second-screen experiences that offer viewers a form of content personalization through their tablets and smartphones in the form of apps. These apps sync to the broadcast in real time, offer "companion content" (e.g., polls, quizzes, and other extra content) and a moderated social stream to communicate with other viewers and program staff, and enable users to share comments on Facebook and Twitter. One example is the app developed for Discovery Channel's *Shark Week* (2011); another is the NBC Live co-viewing app, also released in 2011, for four of its shows, which offered interactive features (e.g., a social stream) and additional original content for viewers watching live episodes.

Similarly, 2008 saw the rapid emergence of entertainment check-in apps such as GetGlue (later TVTag), Philo, Miso, and BeeTV. The goal of these applications was to encourage appointment television by making the consumption of media more social through interactivity. Furthermore, viewers were encouraged to "check in" to the media they were consuming, and, for doing so, they would receive rewards like points, badges, and stickers. By late 2014, most of these apps had proved unable to gain enough audience traction to be viable, and their services were discontinued.

Integration

The fourth type of relation I identify is integration, which is informed by the idea that with digitization, interactivity is increasingly woven into a television program (Gripsrud 2010). Relevant here are not only various real-time voting mechanisms but also the way that comments posted on social media platforms affect onscreen action. Integration differs from overlay in that these online comments are used as direct input for the show.

The four different relations between television and social media I have distinguished here have been developed as part of producers' efforts to help television maintain its centrality in the media landscape, by encouraging users to return to the linear programming of broadcast television. Parsing out these relations reveals what is different about "social TV" as compared to the popular concepts "transmedia storytelling" (Jenkins 2003; Jenkins 2006), "cross-media" (Davidson 2010), or "deep media" (Rose 2012), in that it combines television with the real-time afforded by social media platforms in a number of different ways. To return to the case study that I now consider in depth: although *The Voice* can be understood as either "transmedia storytelling" or as a "cross-media" or "deep media" format, none of these terms fully captures what the show has done—because these concepts, focusing on how social media platforms extend the lived relationship *outside* of the broadcast time slot, do not consider relations such as overlay, enveloping, or integration.

The Voice's Metatext: From Authenticity to Participation

Having considered common narratives about social TV, and having delineated the various possible relations between social media and television, I now turn to *The Voice* and analyze its constellation of liveness: its domains of metatext, space of participation, and user response.

Like many television talent shows in the United States, *The Voice* (in 2016 in its tenth season) purports to uphold "the American Dream." The show is "life changing"—so say its promoters, hosts, judges, and of course its contestants, who, coming from all walks of life, have been given the opportunity to be recognized for their talent. By sharing the conviction that exposure on television can advance the social standing of those featured onscreen, everyone involved with the show acknowledges the power of broadcast television. *The Voice*, however, has sought to differentiate itself from its competitors: it employs blind auditions, so that its contestants can be judged on the basis of their voices rather than looks (hence the title of the program), and it has played the social TV card heavily, casting itself as the most interactive show on television.

The first season of *The Voice*, in 2011, was hosted by Carson Daly. He was joined by four celebrity coaches: musicians Blake Shelton, Cee Lo Green, Christina Aguilera, and Adam Levine. The role of the coach was to assemble a team and tutor its members throughout the competition. In addition, Alison Haislip held the rather distinctive function of "social media correspondent." The program's inclusion of this function highlights the centrality that social media were supposed to have in the format. Season 1 comprised three phases: the blind auditions, the battle rounds, and the live shows.

To outline the metatext of the show, I use information taken from the official NBC website for *The Voice*, the show's press releases for season 1, elements in the episodes themselves (including the implementation of social media by the producers), and online exposés on the show for which representatives were interviewed. As I highlight, the metatext shifted emphasis from authenticity to participation as the show moved from the blind auditions and battle rounds to the live shows.

During the first phase of the show (broadcast in its first two weeks) the coaches selected eight contestants (referred to as "artists") for their teams. With their backs turned away from the stage in their revolving chairs, they listened to the contestants' auditions without seeing them. To pick a particular contestant for their team, a coach pushed a button so that the chair revolved around and faced the performer. In the event that multiple coaches had turned their chairs, the contestant got to pick which team to join.

In the battle rounds (episodes 3–6, broadcast over four weeks) the coaches paired their artists to compete in performances. Each coach had to select the winner for the round, and by the end of this phase all teams had been narrowed down to four contestants. The live shows, in the third phase of the program (during the remaining four weeks of the season), had three segments—the quarter-finals, semi-finals, and finales—each spanning two episodes.

In a press release announcing the program, *The Voice* declared itself "the most digitally integrated show on TV." The media picked up the statement and both Daly and Haislip repeated it on air. The thirty-two contestants who passed the blind auditions were introduced to the possibilities of social media. They each had a blog, Facebook page, Twitter account, video blog, and photo blog, where they shared their experiences of being part of the show (Drell 2011).[57] In this manner, *The Voice* offered its viewers, aside from the television broadcasts themselves, multiple narrative pathways into the *Voice*-verse. The NBC.com homepage featured links to the show's social platforms, provided "24/7 storytelling and continu[ed] all of the reality stories and experiences of the artists and the coaches and the rivalries between them" (Drell 2011, n.p.). The shows' producers were active on the website, Facebook, and Twitter, not only between airings but also in the lead-up to the season and well after the season finale.

Drawing on the taxonomy I have introduced above, I would argue that these program features contribute to what I have called program "extension," as they allowed for the connection between audience and format to extend beyond the show's broadcast timeframe.

The Blind Auditions and Battle Rounds

The first words to be uttered on *The Voice* were those of host Carson Daly. He said, "Welcome to *The Voice*—a singing competition unlike any other because it puts vocal ability first." Here we see the first feature by which the show attempted to differentiate itself from other singing competitions. The fact that the auditions were done blind was also highly emphasized during the first two phases of the competition, addressed not only in the show's surrounding rhetoric but also reproduced within the show itself through sound bites from contestants and the show's judges and hosts. They all claimed the show was different, because it centered on people's voices rather than their looks. A related strategy was to call the contestants "artists" and to refer to the judges as "coaches," thus suggesting a mentor-student relation between them. Whereas the first phase laid claim to authenticity through the blind auditions, the purported authenticity of the battle rounds was put forth through the clips that showcased the coaches mentoring their team members.

With respect to social media, the first two rounds of *The Voice* employed a shared set of uses and functions. For this reason, I elaborate on only one episode as an exemplary instance of social media use in the blind auditions and the battle rounds more generally. The first time a tweet was used on *The Voice* was during the first episode, when one appeared on the screen as an overlay just as contestant Patrick Thomas, after his audition, was supposed to choose among the three coaches that had spun their chairs around for him. Before he was asked to make his choice, the coaches offered feedback on the audition, which led to a discussion between Levine and Shelton (who had both pushed for him). At this time, users were asked to "tweet along with our coaches" and the show's official hashtag #TheVoice was featured onscreen as a call to action. A tweet from Shelton directed at what Levine had just said was then used as an overlay.

Throughout the episode, viewers were encouraged to tweet along with Daly or one of the coaches. As in the example above, only tweets from the show's hosts and coaches were used as overlays. The tweets by Daly, for instance, welcomed contestants to the battle rounds. The official hashtag #The-Voice was strategically placed throughout the episodes in hopes that a community of interest would organize around it. Intended as a coordinating mechanism for Twitter discussions about the show, "#TheVoice" was placed on the screen so as to instruct users to include the hashtag when tweeting about the show.[58]

Social media correspondent Haislip made her first appearance on *The Voice* in the final minutes of this episode. She reported from backstage and introduced herself as a "guide to all that is digitally awesome at *The Voice.*" In this segment, she encouraged viewers to participate and drew their attention to the official website and the show's presence in Apple's iTunes store. As she spoke, an overlay at the bottom third of the screen told viewers to tweet using the designated hashtag and provided her Twitter username, @alisonhaislip. The segment ended with her summing up the multiple ways to stay connected with *The Voice*, 24/7.

Both the blind auditions and the battle rounds were concerned with setting up social media use and creating awareness among the audience of activity outside of the broadcast, particularly on Twitter. These efforts, characterized earlier in this chapter as "enveloping," here involved the posting of commentary from cast members on Twitter, the dissemination of the hashtag on air, and the explanation from Haislip about the other platforms that were part of the format. As noted, the overlays were limited to tweets by the show's hosts and coaches. In general, the use of social media was modest, especially when compared to the live shows.

The Live Shows

Daly's words during the first live show of *The Voice* mark an explicit shift in the program's rhetoric and digital media implementation: "And starting tonight, you at home get a shot at saving one artist on each team." Whereas the metatext for the blind auditions and battle rounds had emphasized authenticity, the metatext of the live shows centered on online connectivity and audience participation. This shift was apparent also in the introduction of what the show called the V-Room, the side stage from which social media correspondent Haislip reported.

The metatext of the live shows heavily stressed the program's new "live" status—even, as I discuss when considering user responses, to the degree that viewers were wondering why Daly was repeatedly stating that the show was live. Included in Daly's call to participation was the construction of the audience as an "imagined community" (Anderson 2006). This was most explicit in how, throughout the live shows, he repeatedly called upon "America" to vote and tweet. Moreover, from the live shows onward, the relation between social media and television was no longer simply one of enveloping, extension, or the overlaying of tweets by hosts and coaches. Now, social media comments from viewers were being used as overlays and integrated into the episodes.

The V-Room, sponsored by Sprint, was the center of this online social activity. Haislip explained its role to the audience as follows:

> This is the V-room. This is where viewers can connect live, right here right now with teams Blake and Christina in so many different ways. First, let's talk Twitter. You can Tweet the artists directly at their personal Twitter handles. Just go to @NBCTheVoice/artists and all the artists are listed there, so hit them up with your questions and comments and make sure to include in your tweet #TheVoice. You are getting a direct line to these guys. Or you can post your comments on the Voice Facebook page and online at nbc.com/thevoice. The artists will be here throughout the show to answer your burning questions. The coaches will be responding as well, so stay connected!

With the live shows, Haislip checked in not just once (as she had during the blind auditions and battle rounds) but multiple times per episode. During these check-ins Haislip commented on online buzz (e.g., with comments like "Twitter is

Fig. 4:   A snapshot of the V-Room (from season 1, episode 12 of *The Voice***)**

blowing up right now" and mentions of contestants trending on Twitter) and explained the multiple ways of connecting *directly* to *The Voice* (e.g., on Twitter and Facebook and via NBC.com) and the artists. Moreover, Haislip would respond to viewer comments and questions, which she read from her tablet.

Analyzing the role of the V-Room, captured in figure 4, brings forward two uses of social media: a bridging of the on-air and online spheres, and the forging of a relationship with the home audience. With regard to the former, the cutaway to the V-Room was explained as a means to "see what's happening online." A sharp distinction was drawn in the metatext between the on-air and online worlds. The V-Room gave online user activity a more tangible, physical form through a web wall with crawling tweets and physical monitors displaying Facebook pages and the NBC.com site. Tweets were featured during check-ins with the V-Room, although Haislip did not interact with the crawling tweets displayed in the lower portion of the screen. Every contestant in the V-Room had a tablet at hand, and Haislip's conversations with the candidates in the V-Room always touched on how viewers on social media were commenting on a candidate's performance, suggesting that the conversation between contestants and fans was developing "live" during the show.

From the V-Room, it was Haislip's task to keep people informed as to the latest online developments.

In terms of forging a relationship with the home audience, presenters and hosts of broadcast television suggested direct contact with the audience through "para-social interaction" (Horton and Wohl 1956). Here the audience feels as if they are in a reciprocal relation with these media personas, although this relation is in fact one-sided. The use of social media in *The Voice* fulfilled a similar function, and sustained the illusion of viewers actually being connected and being part of the ongoing conversation, thus potentially strengthening the bond between program and audience. Through the extensive use of social media during the live shows, *The Voice* proposed that actual communication with the audience was going on via the integrated back-channels of social media. To sustain this illusion, Haislip even asked the contestants questions that viewers had posted online. However, for most viewers not engaged with social media during the show's live broadcast, the interaction with the program, its cast, and other viewers continued to be an imagined construct, as in traditional para-social interaction. Outside of the V-Room, moreover, social media were referenced only through a strategically placed hashtag.

Taken together, the live show's metatext and its social media use were involved in the construction of event TV—a kind to be watched now rather than later. By incorporating social media activity, the program acknowledged the home audience so as to make it part of a conversation, in the process underscoring again the significance of the broadcast. Haislip reported which *Voice* topics were trending on Twitter, thus highlighting the idea that a lot was happening around the program online. This can be read not only as a "hook into this sense of real-time and urgency" (Halperin 2011, n.p.) but also as confirming the liveness of the broadcast, with liveness being a marker of importance.

The Live Shows' Space of Participation

Having analyzed the metatext, I now delineate the space of participation for the live shows. *The Voice* was developed as a format with multiple spaces of participation, which were tied together by the telecast. There were, first off, multiple media by which viewers could cast votes on a contestant or contestants. Furthermore, the real-time experience of Twitter, Facebook, and the NBC.com website extended and even transformed this domain when it was channeled into the show. However, as opposed to what celebratory accounts of participatory television would have us believe, the live shows remained a producer-controlled space with viewers who had very limited impact on what unfolded onscreen. It seems that user participation was harvested around the program and was occasionally pulled in to help stimulate the illusion of para-social interaction. Here I touch briefly on these peripheral spaces, because they co-shaped the space of participation of *The Voice*'s format as a whole.

I should note in advance that *The Voice*, to accommodate the economic imperative at the heart of primetime television in the United States, was first broadcast on the East Coast and then re-aired three hours later on the West Coast.[59] This practice, known as "tape delay," is used to maximize audience size. A show is aired in the most attractive time slot in all time zones, in order to target particular audience segments and achieve the largest possible exposure. As television has come to incorporate social media in its practice, doubt has been cast as to whether this continues to be a smart strategy for networks, because viewers now complain about the spread of spoilers.

Officially, people couldn't watch *The Voice* outside the United States, because the show wasn't broadcast elsewhere. Within the country, some people couldn't watch because they couldn't receive over-the-air television signals and didn't have a cable subscription. However, links to (illegal) online video streams of *The Voice* were shared on Twitter, allowing people to watch the East Coast broadcast of the show "live." In addition, the episodes were available shortly after airings in the form of torrents and streaming video. As such, the official space of participation for the program was extended through illegal practices.

As I explained earlier, relations changed among the show, the cast, and its audience during the live shows. An important difference from earlier rounds of the show was the ability of viewers to now cast votes to help their favorite artists move forward in the competition. Daly repeatedly stressed this transfer of power: "You at home get to choose which artist is saved." In fact, for the quarterfinals and semi-finals, it was the audience votes, in collaboration with the coaches'— weighted fifty/fifty—that determined which contestant moved on to the next round. During the finale, the results of user voting determined the winner.

The Voice offered several voting methods: by phone, online, and through iTunes purchases. However, voting was not available to everyone. Although people had managed to view the show outside the United States, which was evident from online comments, audience participation through voting was officially restricted through the "Voting Terms and Conditions" that defined the geographical parameters for voting. Toll-free telephone voting and online voting was open only to people located in the United States and Puerto Rico.

On iTunes, geography also played a role, as geo-filtering prevented people from accessing the U.S. store outside its designated territory; thus, those people could not purchase the contestant songs there that had been performed during the show and would count toward that week's vote count. Inside the voting window, the songs were available for download through the U.S. iTunes Store, but were released to an international audience only after the voting window had closed. Moreover, downloading a song from iTunes cost $1.29. The price introduced an economic barrier to this particular method of voting, complementing the technological hurdle of the required iTunes software. The voting window via all three methods, however, was fairly long. Viewers would still be able to vote even if watching the show several hours or even days later than the original broadcast.

The NBC.com website served primarily as an extension of the broadcast. Here all thirty-two contestants who had made it to the second round were featured with links to their blogs, Facebook pages, Twitter accounts, video blogs, and photo blogs. Taken together, these provided viewers multiple ways of accessing the show's narrative. The website also included "web exclusive" content, like videos, though geo-filtering made such content accessible only from an IP address inside the United States.

The social media strategy for the first season of *The Voice* focused primarily on Twitter and Facebook. These platforms allowed for enveloping of the program and the on-air integration of social media comments. In both cases, watching live was an important prerequisite. Each live-show episode overlaid several user tweets and posed two or so questions that had been posted to Facebook or on NBC.com. Although the show's producers had hoped to incorporate other social networks as well, the necessity of negotiations for use of each specific post from these other social networks prevented them from doing so (Edelsburg 2011). This is an obvious way in which legal forces, by limiting which social media comments could be used on the show, helped shape the format's space of participation.

In light of Twitter's central role in the program, I need to briefly address its particular space of participation.[60] With regard to *The Voice*, Twitter enabled audience members to connect not only with one another but also with the program's cast members. Simply put, Twitter is a microblogging service that facilitates the sending and reading of text-based messages of up to 140 characters. Unless its default settings are changed, a tweet is publicly visible. The platform allows users to subscribe to the tweets of others in a practice known as "following." Consequently, all the tweets from the people whom the user follows are collected in a stream on their Twitter homepage (and can also be viewed via popular Twitter apps such as TweetDeck). It accommodates several forms of social interaction. One is "mass-self communication" (Castells 2009), meaning that individuals can disseminate messages to a potentially mass audience. It is also possible to set up conversations about or directed at individuals. This is done by including that person's username in a tweet, preceded by the "@" symbol. Such a tweet will appear on the sender's profile page. Furthermore, if the recipient is a follower of the sender, the tweet will appear in that user's timeline view (visible to all),[61] but not on his or her profile page. However, if the recipient is not following the sender, the tweet can still be found via the @mentions tab. It is possible to post messages by topic through the use of hashtags (#). First employed by Twitter's users, hashtags are a cultural shorthand enabling communities of interest to emerge around a given topic by prefixing a word with a pound sign.

The official hashtag for *The Voice* allowed the show's fans to find and interact with one another. Part of the excitement in tweeting, and in doing so enveloping the broadcast, lay in the possibility that a representative of the show might reply to the tweet or that it might appear on air.[62] However, it was a challenge for the show's producers to integrate real-time Twitter commentary into the live broadcast. For instance, it took about fifteen seconds to get tweets on air because they had to meet several standards and pass through legal filtering (Drell 2011). Furthermore, Twitter's recommendation on the use of tweets in a broadcast was, as I discovered through tallying them, to have a large percentage of the featured tweets be from the cast (in this case, coaches and/or contestants) rather than the audience. In other words, legal and cultural factors reduced the likelihood that viewer comments would be overlaid on the screen or otherwise integrated on air during the broadcast.

Twitter's role as an envelope or extension to the broadcast made it also possible to @mention the show's host, coaches, or contestants, particularly as their Twitter usernames were promoted on air and on the show's website. The sheer volume of messages directed at these individuals, however, stood in the way even of responding, let alone building relationships. Clay Shirky (2009) would call this an example of "cognitive limits," which force popular people on the Web into non-reciprocal, one-way relationships. Indeed, the cast members of *The Voice* were unable to reciprocate the attention they received and were forced to maintain a one-to-many mode of communication. Interestingly, users, understanding the problem, asked to be re-tweeted or to be followed on Twitter (or both), or to have their Facebook comments liked instead.

User Responses: Different Constructions of the Live

Having reflected on the metatext and the space of participation of *The Voice*, I now explore five different constructions in its constellation of the live: live television, watching live, live-tweeting, live performance, and live audience. These constructs are identifiable thanks mainly but not exclusively to user responses. These responses help me consider how viewers reflected on the liveness of the show and explore the conditions in which liveness comes into effect. The metatext does not explicitly reflect on these notions because it simply helps inform the meaning and values that materialize in the larger constellation; it is less common for any of them to be singled out.

To determine how the term "live" was used in relation to the show, I consider what was tweeted during the four two-hour episodes at the end of the season: episodes eight, nine, eleven, and the finale. The tweets were gathered by taking a snapshot, once every five minutes, during a broadcast of the feed in Monitter (a web-based tool for real-time Twitter monitoring), set to compile those tweets that mentioned both "TheVoice" and "live." This resulted in a collection of 658 unique tweets sent out during the show's East Coast broadcast, plus another 38 collected from the final results show when it was broadcast later on the West Coast.[63]

Live Television

With the live shows, as I have mentioned several times, the relationship between the audience and the format was redefined. This change entailed that the emphasis of the metatext shifted from authenticity to participation, and that social media use in and around the program exploded. In relation to the "live" associated with the construct of "live television," the user responses highlight four important points.

First, live television was understood here as content broadcast in (more or less) real time mixed with prerecorded content. The disclaimer "portions prerecorded" at the beginning of each of the live-show episodes drew attention to this fact. The episodes in their entirety, however, were identified as "live," not only because they were called "live shows," but because they were consistently referred to and discussed as such on the official website and by the show's representatives. Among the Twitter users, no one complained about or even commented on the fact that portions of the show had been prerecorded. One reason that this was overlooked or simply taken in stride may be that prior to most performances, and in support of the show's general disclaimer, the word "LIVE" would be subtly superimposed in the top left corner of the screen for a few seconds. So although the live shows were themselves framed as "live," it seems that this liveness needed to be emphasized during the performances. This created hierarchies of value within the live shows—without, however, eclipsing the general appreciation of these shows as "live."

Second, the use of tape delay for the West Coast broadcast reveals something about the Twitter users' understanding of live television. While the mix of prerecorded material with live material was understood still to be live television, the tape delay did create some conflict among the audience. Viewers on the West Coast took issue with Daly's use of the term "live."[64] For instance, @Inspired_Panda tweeted:

> @bitchcraftradio because it isn't live on the west coast (aired earlier on the east coast) #thevoice

The issue of tape delay is addressed in greater depth later in this chapter. For now, it is sufficient to point out that live-tweeting put new pressures on the liveness of the broadcasts.

Third, live television is explored in the tweets as a socially constructed space for self-monitoring. Toward the end of the second live-round episode, for instance, Becca Zielinski noted the following on Twitter:

> Hey Carlson Daly, is #thevoice live?...how many times are you gonna remind us? Probably gotta remind @blakeshelton so he watches his mouth.

Not only does this statement make clear that liveness was strongly emphasized in the metatext, it also jokingly suggests that Daly's repetition was necessary to keep Shelton from using profanity on the air. This reveals that live television was perceived as a space that required self-monitoring. Not surprisingly, a popular topic on Twitter concerned what the coaches and hosts could and couldn't say or do on live television. During a live show in 2013, Levine muttered, "I hate this country," resulting in online public fury. The incident suggested that NBC did not implement a five-second delay for the live telecasts.

Such an understanding surfaced in the program itself, too. In the second live-show episode, for example, following a provocative comment by Levine, Daly tapped his microphone twice and said, "Hello. Hello. Are we still live?" then double-tapped the microphone again to test if it was on. Jokingly done, yes, but it referred to the fact that television (network television in particular) requires some self-monitoring because on-air conduct is shaped by cultural norms. In fact, federal law prohibits expressions of what it deems indecency or profanity between 6 AM and 10 PM on network television, and the broadcast time of *The Voice* fell into this timeslot. The Federal Communications Commission (FCC) is responsible for enforcing indecency regulations and imposes penalties for violations. Prerecorded television gives broadcasters more control in selecting what material to air, whereas live television requires that the people on air be more self-conscious with respect to what they say and do. Many networks therefore opt to broadcast with five-second delays for much of their live programming, to prevent unwanted material from being sent over the airwaves uncensored.

The fourth and final aspect of the live in live television, made evident through tweets on the topic, is how live television is used as a platform to address "the nation" about matters of social significance. Earlier, in my consideration of the live shows' metatext, I argued that its address to the collective and its social media use underscored its significance. In line with this observation, two incidents that occurred during *The Voice*'s live shows revealed forces that favor a centralized media system. In the first case, because of President Obama's primetime address to the country, the results show was aired ten minutes later than planned.[65] In announcing the interruption of scheduled programming, Daly suggested that this should only happen if something was *even more* important than *The Voice*: "If *The Voice* should be delayed for someone it should be for the President—let's get to it" (he later thanked President Obama while signing off the episode). Here we see highlighted television's continued central importance (Gripsrud 2010) or, to make this statement more nuanced, its *perceived* importance.

The second incident was the interruption, on June 21, 2011, of the Eastern and Central Daylight Time broadcast so that tornado watches for the Central Plains could be spread over the airwaves. A tweet from Tiffany Bailey, echoing popular online sentiment, casts light on the meaning of live television:

> Weather service I need you to stop interrupting #TheVoice to talk about this tornado watch. I get it, but my show is on live, let me live!

The tornado watches created some frustration among audience members because, as a live television show, *The Voice* unfolded in real time and could not be paused. Part of the audience missed several minutes of the episode as a result of the tornado watch. Both the president's address and the tornado-watch interruption suggest that centralized media is necessary for matters of regional or national concern. However, a tweet like the one cited above suggests that there is no consensus about what is important enough to warrant such alterations in scheduled programming.

Watching Live

The construct of live television is linked to the practice of watching live. Live watching concerns the status of the transmission rather than the status of what is broadcast (as is the case with live television). Here, I examine audience reflections on the topic through tweets about watching *The Voice* "live," and reflect on audience size.

The tweets I collected show a polarized audience experience arising around the theme of watching live. For Jared Varner, watching television live was marked by the burden of having to watch advertisements:

> First time watching #thevoice live. Now I remember why. I hate commercials!

This is just one tweet out of many that addressed the disadvantage of watching television live and the loss of control that comes with it. But not everyone shared this sentiment. Erin Knight, in contrast, stressed the advantage of live watching:

#TheVoice has made watching TV live relevant again! #SorryDVR This show is so much fun!

So whereas watching live entailed the drawbacks of less viewer control and the necessity of watching advertisements, many viewers, nonetheless, seemed to be excited about being able to watch the show live.

The season 1 finale of *The Voice* attracted five percent of U.S. households (roughly 10.5 million viewers), which is significantly less than some of the larger television events nowadays. Moreover, the live shows received, on average, an audience share comparable to those of the blind-audition and battle-round shows. In combination with the tweets discussed both here and previously (to explore live television), these facts underscore that the index "live," although perceived to be a value, does not guarantee that viewers will necessarily tune in.

Live-tweeting

Another central construction in the live show's constellation came up in relation to tweeting. To explore this construction, I briefly discuss tweeting as an activity that enveloped the broadcast, then examine two problems to which live-tweeting draws attention.

Research conducted by Pew Research Center, a nonpartisan organization that conducts empirical social science research on media consumption (among other things), found that, as of May 2011, thirteen percent of adults online were using Twitter (Bergman 2011a). Data on *The Voice* are hard to come by, but online publications reveal that the first live episode generated some 200,000 *Voice*-related tweets (see Halperin 2011).[66] That 12.31 million people watched the episode helps us to understand which share of the viewers was actually producing online chatter. Even if we assume that each tweet represented a unique viewer, this would mean that only 1.6 percent of the viewers tweeted during the show—and that at least 98.4 percent of viewers were not tweeting.[67] Such quantitative ratios, of course, say nothing about the nature of what this minority of viewers tweeted. Moreover, it remains unclear how many people were *exposed* to tweets while watching the broadcast (reading them, but not tweeting themselves).

To gain insight into the Twitter activity around *The Voice*, I used the tool Trendistic, which traces the frequency of a topic on Twitter over a period of thirty days.[68] Tracing the transition period from the battle rounds to the live shows made it possible to make the following observations. To begin with, the tweet frequency peaked in activity during the original broadcasts, which confirms the idea that social TV is especially oriented toward participation *during* the broadcast timeframe. Moreover, these Twitter spikes show an explosion of tweet activity when the live shows kicked off. Compared to the battle rounds, the percentage of tweets mentioning the show tripled. This suggests that the shift found in the metatext and the expansion of the space of participation corresponds to more Twitter mentions—a combination which in turn underscores the participatory character of the live shows.

Analyzing the tweets that mention the term "TheVoice" on the day of the first live show (episode 8) produced some interesting insights into Twitter activity,[69] which peaked just after 9 PM, at the beginning of the initial East Coast broadcast.[70] It then descended, and then began slightly inclining again at the start of the West Coast airing. After about an hour, it started declining again, and three hours later the number of tweets about the show returned to pre-broadcast levels. This once again confirms that online conversation is concentrated around airings.

Reading tweets around these episodes revealed conflict between East and West Coast viewers—an issue that has received scholarly attention before (Deller 2011). Specifically, members of the West Coast audience were frustrated that members of the East Coast audience were tweeting spoilers. They demanded that viewers watching the original broadcast elsewhere in the country stop revealing outcomes. The problem reached a climax in the finale episode. Matthew Senna's tweet expressed the position that social media and television shows would always clash unless shows were actually broadcast "live":

> #thevoice ruined the results by not having a live finale. With social media you can't keep results secret for 3hrs!

This was further underscored in a tweet by Diana, who had problems with the show's rhetoric—a point that has also surfaced in my discussion of watching live:

> WTH MAN! These lives [*sic*] shows aren't really live! People need to keep their mouths shut until each time zone watches the show #TheVoice

The above tweets question the applicability of the index "live" for the re-airing. It makes clear that the label cannot be asserted simply on the basis of the metatext alone—an argument I made in chapter 4, where users took issue with the claim that eJamming was being promoted as live.

The spoiler problem in relation to tape delay and the real time of social media is not limited to live-tweeting in the United States. There are many other countries that also span multiple time zones (e.g., Canada, Russia, and Australia). Syndication delays have strained the relationship among audiences from different countries as well, as spoilers circulate online (see Bergman 2011a). However, the problem has changed now that programs are *encouraging* users to go online. The following tweet by Aaron Egaas makes this clear:

> Hey live TV shows, don't tell your west coasters to go on Twitter only to have your show spoiled. #fail #theVoice #fail

In relation to strategies of enveloping, the "clash of the coasts" problem has been met in different ways. Some social apps make a distinction between the two audience groups, allowing users to select either the Eastern or Pacific discussion. Another strategy has been to use different hashtags for the two. More drastically, awards shows like the Golden Globes, the Academy Awards, and the Emmy Awards have opted to broadcast live coast-to-coast on account of the proliferation of real-time social media. Later, I return to this topic (specifically as it relates to Twitter), because it highlights a tension surrounding the live: broadcasters' control over the schedules, I argue, conflicts here with the audience's desire to participate. My reflections on the topic should in turn help to grasp the standing of broadcast television in the social media era.

As for the conversation that took place on Twitter, a qualitative analysis reveals that the forms of social interaction emerging here are distinct from traditional conceptions of water-cooler conversation around television. The audience could now address the hosts, coaches, or contestants either by tweeting at them or mentioning them in a tweet. In spite of this, most of the tweets consisted of commentary and amounted to a form of mass self-communication rather than dialogue.[71] Except for some very modest re-tweet activity, viewers were not reacting to one another (although the sheer volume of tweets might well prevent me from establishing this claim with absolute certainty—even when filtering by hashtag, tracking actual conversations around popular topics in real time is an all but impossible task). Haislip's reference to online activity as "buzz" thus aptly characterizes Twitter activity alongside television.

Bruns and Stieglitz write the following about the role of hashtags, when Twitter functions as a back-channel for live events:

> [A] sense of temporary, imagined community persists even if—as our data show—actual direct interaction between users through hashtagged @replies and retweets remains relatively rare; it may be sufficient to observe the stream of hashtagged comments, even without engaging with and replying to them. (Bruns and Stieglitz 2012, 177)

Bruns and Stieglitz here describe in general terms what I have observed in relation specifically to *The Voice*. I would add, moreover, that the incorporation of selected tweets onscreen in a ticker, as has been done in *The Voice*, enhances the sense of community they write about. It could therefore be argued that social media were instrumental in constructing *The Voice*'s episodes as must-see TV.

Considering the number of *The Voice* cast members' Twitter followers allows for a final observation to be made on the relation between social media and television. Comparing data before and after *The Voice* shows that Adam Levine, Cee Lo Green, and Blake Shelton almost tripled their followers on Twitter during the show's first season, with noticeable rises after airings.[72] The following of Javier Colon, the winner of season 1, grew exponentially: his 743 followers two days before the beginning of the show increased to 60,882 on the day of the finale.[73] The popular discourse on social TV tends to frame the relationship between these media only in terms of how it benefits television. The above numbers, however, suggest that the relationship is also beneficial to Twitter.[74]

Live Performance

Having addressed the constructions of live television, watching live, and live-tweeting, I now explore the construct of live performance. To do so, I return to the metatext's rhetoric of authenticity and discuss the role of live performance in promoting this value. I also look at how the audience wrote about the "live" in live performances on blogs and in tweets.

Throughout season 1, the coaches commented on the contestants' performances. On several occasions, a coach would praise a performance by noting that singing that particular song live was not easy. Here, obviously, live performance was being valued over the making of a recording in a studio. More specifically, a live performance, such statements suggest, allows for a better evaluation of a performer's talent.

Tweets echoed the judges' perception that live performances are particularly difficult and are the best way to assess someone's talent. Mitchell Holder, for instance, claimed that

> Adam Levine is a talentless live singing sham. Pales in comparison to the other coaches. #TheVoice

Alice Welch retweeted @SwiftyGuy13, who used the comparison between studio recording and live performance to assert the value of the latter:

> RT @ SwiftyGuy13: Blake sounds as good live as he does in studio. Not many artists can do that! #TheVoice

This statement implicitly references the idea that studio recordings are the product of extensive polishing of artists' voices. Live performance, by contrast, is done without the help of studio equipment. The definition of a good live performance, by implication, is one that sounds like a studio recording, but is achieved without the aid of post-production fixes. These ideas also imply that live performance is the optimal means to evaluate the talent or quality of an artist. The coaches' repeated comments about how certain songs are particularly difficult to perform live further reinforce this logic.

Tweets about the performances made available on iTunes also make clear that live performance holds the promise that the singing is taking place now, as the show is being broadcast—and that the artist is not lip-syncing a recording. This is evident from the question being raised of how it was possible that the recordings of the contestants' performances offered through iTunes were already available online before their songs had been performed on the show.[75]

Jethro Nededog (2011), a reporter from the online magazine Zap2it, wrote a short review of the show's taping that helps to further understand the value attributed to live performance. Nededog made the interesting disclosure that a performance by the coaches was taped:

> Yes, it was mostly live (as coach Adam Levine's S-bomb proved), but the judges pre-taped their Queen medley right before the show went live. We don't blame them. After all, they're not competing. As for the actual performers, we can vouch for all of them—*that was live.* (my emphasis)

There are several observations to be drawn here. To begin with, live performance is defined here as something that has not been prerecorded. This is linked to my discussion of the notion of live television, where I suggested that the use of obscene language proves that a show has not been prerecorded or edited. Something similar also happens with live performance, which is seen to carry risks that non-live performance does not. In addition, Nededog's need to vouch for the contestants' performances as really being "live" underscores the importance of them doing so on "live" television. That he is sympathetic to the coaches having their performances prerecorded highlights this even more. It reveals, also, how the live dimension of the show is appreciated as being necessary for the competition, because it allows the show to reveal whether a contestant's talent is authentic.

Live Audience

The live in the live audience construct is closely akin to the live in live performance. The live audience concerns the people present at the tapings or airings of *The Voice*. Some of these audience members made themselves known online, blogging about their experience and/or live-tweeting extra content. In addition, *The Hollywood Reporter* was present at the tapings and published reports on the show on its website, accompanied by the slogan "THR's Live Feed was there, here's what you didn't see on TV."

As mentioned in chapter 3, Scannell (2001) argues that in a televised event there are actually two "events," each with a distinct audience: the event and its crowd, and the television coverage of the event and those who watch it on their screens. The coverage offers a perspective of the event that is very different from that of any individual present there. Scannell criticizes those that claim that television is somehow inauthentic because of its selectivity and its constructedness. To him, the event being broadcast is equally a construction and is therefore by no means more authentic than its representation on television. Having examined the blogs and tweets of *The Voice*, however, one must acknowledge that the "events" in question are connected, and that being present at the taping gives one a privileged relation to the show. This is probably because the live audience has comparatively more control over their experience of it.

Some Conditions of the Live

The various constructs discussed above, all emerging together in the constellation of liveness at play in the *The Voice*'s live shows, allow for several observations on how liveness takes effect. Generally speaking, to make inferences about a specific live construct taking shape, one clearly requires an understanding of its context. Let me clarify this point through a comparison. Bars frequently advertise upcoming "live soccer" events on posters and banners. People know, of course, that there will be no actual soccer match inside the bar, but rather that a broadcast of the match will be shown on a large screen. However, were they to advertise "live music," these same people would expect there to be at least one musician and probably a band performing on stage (and would not assume, for instance, that they would have to listen to a live broadcast of a musical performance on the radio or television). In the former instance, it is known that "live" refers to a broadcast; in the latter, people can anticipate that it refers to an actual performance. Reflecting on the various types of liveness found in *The Voice*'s live shows, it becomes similarly apparent that the context and consequently the reference point for the "live" is absolutely crucial to understanding it. Think, for example, of my claim that hierarchies of value were created within the episodes whenever distinctions were made between live and non-live aspects of the live shows. Likewise, it is important to know here whether, if using the term "live," someone is referring to the show at large or to a particular segment.

Based on my consideration of the live constructions present in the show, I would propose that each construction is a particular articulation of how the format interacted with its audience(s). In their combined operation, these constructions existed within, but also gave shape to, the overarching space of participation that coalesced for the live shows. Participatory practices ranged from being present at the taping, watching it live, and live-tweeting it to staying connected through other platforms that offered insights into the program around the airings. However, several other sorts of interactions were possible within the shows' space of participation, which were not identified as "live" (e.g., voting, downloading songs from iTunes, and doing non-real-time activities on the NBC website). This demonstrates again that live constructs, resulting from very different spatial and temporal configurations, vary in meaning.

Another insight coincides with a (gradual) shift in the focus of this book, manifesting itself in this chapter, from interest in what I have sometimes called the "paradox of liveness" (which relates to the live's fundamental *constructedness*) to an exploration of the conditions and operation of specific live constellations. Based on the exploration of the five live constructions in this chapter, and relating those to the previous chapter, I can propose the following non-exhaustive list of conditions of the live:

1. "Live" is used as an adjective to describe the properties of a given noun. The noun and the context inform the meaning of the adjective "live."
2. "Live" is seemingly always contrasted to a "non-live" counterpart, and its meaning is informed by that contrast.
3. "Live" is a qualitative category. It is used as a source of distinction (Levine 2008).
4. "Live" propels certain values by drawing on the special relationship between *real time* and *sociality* (although it does so in some cases as a connection to an event/ performance rather than to other people).

With regard to this fourth point, this chapter reinforces my observation that liveness is built around a special relationship between sociality and real-time experience. But it also shows that in different constellations of liveness, these axes are articulated in different ways. So therefore, the sociality offered on one platform differs from that of another.

The conditions of the live apply in the cases of the specific constructions of the live that I have discussed, but also within the broader, overarching constellation of the live shows. *The Voice*'s live show constellation, of course, was informed by the multiple constructs that articulated specific relations to the format, which means that multiple references for the term "live" were relevant for the show. But additionally, the show as such contrasted the live shows with the blind auditions and battle rounds (which were prerecorded and presented relatively limited opportunities for audience participation). In the process, the live shows were framed as being superior to the blind auditions and battle rounds—indeed, they were positioned as must-see event TV. From this phase in the competition onward, the show as such became "live," and with this evolution a more expansive space of participation took shape.

Tension Surrounding the Live: The Rhythms and Temporalities of Broadcast Television

Having analyzed the constellation of liveness of *The Voice*'s live shows, I want to zoom in now on a tension surrounding the live that clearly manifests itself in that constellation, a tension that relates to, or emerges from, the rhythms and temporalities of television. The tension first came to light in my discussion of user responses. As television was complemented with social media, the liveness of the broadcast came under question, as the live episodes of *The Voice* were re-aired, three hours later, for West Coast viewers. This issue can be related to a larger transformation taking place in the social media era, namely a shift in the relationship between the television industry and its "empowered" viewers. I propose here that even in the social media era, scheduling functions as a mechanism of control, a way that media institutions exert their dominance over the production and distribution of media content. Such control supports the symbolic power of the media—that is, the power to define social reality.

In recent decades, technologies such as video-on-demand (VOD) have allowed viewers to challenge the schedules provided by broadcasters, enabling them to watch content at their own convenience, and in the process upsetting the long-established business model for broadcast television. Broadcasters' control had already been slipping, with the introduction first of remote controls and later of videocassette recorders (followed by DVR). These technologies, which help "free" viewers from broadcast schedules, have fueled the need for broadcasters to develop strategies such as social TV to encourage appointment viewing.

Jenkins et al. (2013) have argued that the television industry continues to struggle with measuring the value of engagement, as it slowly transitions from an "appointment-based model of television viewing" to an "engagement-based paradigm." In the case of the former, viewers watched programs according to the schedule of the programmers. In the latter instance, the willingness of viewers to pursue content over numerous channels is seen to have market value. But what form of engagement to measure, and what business transactions to construct around these engagements, remains partly undecided.

With social TV, there is a commitment to the appointment-based model. The recent pairing of television with social media, however, has raised important issues as to what is at stake in having people participate in and around the media process. *The Voice* brings to light a tension surrounding the live between the participatory spaces provided by the institutions and the agency of viewers. This tension is at the core of social TV, in that this model is employed as an industry strategy to have people watch programs as they are aired, as opposed to having them shift their time of viewing according to their own needs.

As became apparent in the interaction between television and Twitter, the different temporalities of the media created conflict: West Coast viewers resented viewers further east for having first access to *The Voice*'s performances and results. This raised questions about the institutionalized practice of always airing programs in prime time, and thus re-airing programs on the West Coast hours after they had been broadcast elsewhere. Specifically, as pointed out earlier, there was the problem of "spoilers." Ironically, the threat of spoilers is also what makes social TV an attractive strategy to discourage time-shifting viewing.

This problem is perhaps best explored through Matt Hills's (2002) concept of "just-in-time fandom." The concept refers to the enmeshment of fan practices within the rhythms and temporalities of broadcasting in the digital environment. Clarifying the concept, and reflecting on the implications of the digital environment for fandom, Hills writes:

> Describing the temporality of just-in-time fandom as a techno-evolution towards fuller 'interactivity,' which is deemed superior to the prior 'time-lag' involved in the writing to and reading niche magazines' letter pages,... neglects the extent to which this eradication of the 'time-lag' works even more insistently to discipline and regulate the opportunities for temporally-licensed 'feedback,' and the very horizons of the fan experience. (2002, 179)

Hills discusses just-in-time fandom as the ability of fans to show their dedication, in the digital environment, right after an airing or during commercial breaks; but his statement here seems to anticipate social media platforms, which enable viewers to discuss onscreen action with others while programs are being transmitted. More than a decade after Hills was writing, indeed, social TV aligns the timing of fan response even more closely with the broadcast. Computer-mediated communications, to reformulate Hills, have placed a premium on the timing of fan response—and social media platforms have made its timeframe even more immediate.

Netflix, it could be argued, is emblematic of "new television" in the social media era. Discussion of its VOD service allows me to relate the tension identified here to larger transformations taking place in the media landscape. The platform has made headlines for two strategies that went on to make its name on the market: series dumping, and the use of data in developing original content. These strategies center on the viewing behaviors and values of viewers. It is important to realize that Netflix, rather than having to sell audiences to advertisers, as in the broadcast model, requires that viewers pay for its service on a subscription basis (a service that came out of its subscription-based video-rental business). Although my discussion concerns Netflix specifically, many other platforms have come to adopt its practices.

Series Dumping

The more interesting of these two strategies is Netflix's challenge to established ideas of television seriality. As it did in 2012 with the Norwegian show *Lilyhammer*, Netflix decided in 2013 to release at one time an entire season's episodes of the series *House of Cards* (an original Netflix production) and *Arrested Development* (continued by Netflix after having been cancelled many years earlier by Fox, to the continued disappointment of a loyal fan base), and all episodes up to then of *Breaking Bad* (a five-season series shown on AMC, which also produced it; it was nearing its finale). Netflix thus freed viewers from broadcast schedules, and in doing so encouraged the "binge-watching" of these shows. In this way,

Netflix reduced broadcasters' control over when people consumed television content. But this practice has had other consequences as well. Enabling people to watch episodes back-to-back "has affected the structure and content of shows, allowing scriptwriters to sidestep recaps, cliff-hangers, and similar narrative devices intended to keep viewers glued between commercial breaks and from one week to the next" (Hallinan and Striphas 2014, 13).

Response to the simultaneous release of all a season's episodes at once has not been universally lauded. Writing on the website *Mashable*, Christine Erickson (2013) compared the first four weeks of conversation around *House of Cards* on social media to the average first four weeks of conversation for the season premieres of six other shows from top television networks. Whereas *House of Cards* garnered the highest social buzz at the start of the comparison, the volume quickly dropped and continued to do so over time. By contrast, the other shows managed to create weekly peaks and sustain the conversation over time.

Suzanne Scott was equally cautious with respect to series dumping. In an interview with Jenkins (2013), published on the latter's blog, she pointed to the importance of the gaps and margins of television text for fan culture. Citing Hills's concept of "just-in-time fandom," she suggests that eradicating the time lag between episodes may have negative implications for the pleasures of television fandom. Interestingly, rather than proclaiming that the viewer has been emancipated from the broadcasters' schedules, she finds that in series-dump programs fans are impoverished in their ability to share and engage with a community of peers around the show.

In light of such reflections, it is not surprising that for the premiere of the show *Orange Is the New Black*, released in July 2013, Netflix tweaked its approach. This time around, it managed to sustain and grow online buzz by organizing regular Twitter events that brought actors and audiences in contact with each other, and by mounting a distributed promotional campaign rather than making one large promotional push, although it did not prevent binge-watching (Miller 2013).[76] Similarly, Amazon Studios has released the first three episodes of each of its series *Alpha House* and *Betas* together, finding a middle ground between Netflix's initial approach and that of traditional TV.

Data-driven Decision Making

The second Netflix strategy to be addressed here relates also to the platform's decision, in an effort to differentiate itself from other streaming video sites, to start producing its own original series, like those just mentioned (Baldwin 2012). In taking this step, Netflix tried to establish itself as an online network. The company made headlines because the series *House of Cards* was born of vast number crunching, using data on viewer preferences and habits. As Andrew Leonard remarked:

> Netflix doesn't know merely what we're watching, but when, where and with what kind of device we're watching. It keeps a record of every time we pause the action—or rewind, or fast-forward—and how many of us abandon a show entirely after watching for a few minutes. (Leonard 2013, n.p.)

The algorithms it used determined that there was a potential audience for a show that combined the features of a political thriller, the actor Kevin Spacey, and the style of director David Fincher (Hallinan and Striphas 2014). Amazon Studios has taken a similar but more elaborate route in collecting audience feedback, using a submission system and crowd-sourced responses to test show ideas and determine which ones to bankroll. It has mounted such surveys in addition to crunching data on Amazon purchases and browsing behavior on the Internet Movie Database website (which it owns).

Of course, selecting which series to produce on the basis of data is not new—so it would be inaccurate to cast *House of Cards* as marking a new dawn for television production. However, several things have in fact changed in the social media era: the scale of the data that can be collected and crunched, the steering of users to new content through sophisticated recommendation systems (Keating 2013), and the use of real-time data, which allows for real-time analytics (van Dijck and Poell 2013).

Tension Surrounding the Live: Audience Participation

To return to *The Voice*, there is yet another tension surrounding the live that surfaces in the process of analyzing the program, and specifically in considering how it evolved over time. Gradually, a friction emerged between the multiple spaces of participation for *The Voice* in its different seasons. Although the meaning of liveness stayed intact (as in the Mogulus/Original Livestream case discussed in chapter 3), a noticeable shift took place in the role that social media played in the episodes, along with a transformation of the opportunities for audience participation. So here, rather than a whole new constellation emerging, instead there was friction, which manifested itself over seven seasons as inconsistency in how audience participation was sought out.

To support my observation, let me briefly summarize the changes that took place.[77] In the transition from season 1 to season 2, singer-songwriter Christina Milian replaced V-Correspondent Alison Haislip. She held this position up to and including season 4. After this personnel switch, the focus in the social media segments shifted from the integration of social media comments into the show to backstage-like interviews with the artists. For season 3, the V-Room was traded in for the much smaller, circular Sprint Skybox, located in the middle of the audience bleachers. It featured just one small screen, where most often the Sprint logo was displayed and on occasion particular hashtags were promoted. In this way, social media comments were no longer part of the décor. Also, the viewer comments that were featured on air were increasingly overlays rather than being more fully integrated into the show.

By season 5, the role of social media correspondent had been axed, with host Daly making appearances in the Sprint Skybox to talk to guests and erratically address social media comments (see figure 5). These comments were integrated into the show a bit more frequently later on, but this time they primarily were comments directed at Daly himself or the coaches, rather than at the contestants. Moreover, a new type of integration was introduced for this season: the "instant

Fig. 5: A snapshot of the Sprint Skybox (from season 7, episode 27 of *The Voice*)

save," which enabled viewers to save one of the bottom two contestants from elimination by voting with a tweet. This allowed for a lesser form of influence on the production when compared to the higher influence possible when social media comments were addressed on the show.[78]

In short, the relations among the program, the show's representatives, and the audience were reconfigured to favor the producers—allowing them to more fully control what transpired "live" on air (among other means, by giving viewers only accumulative influence on the production through voting, by limiting the number of viewer questions answered on air, and by directing these questions at Daly or the coaches rather than the contestants, who were less predictable). In this way, the show basically retreated from interacting substantively with the audience through social media on air.

In the way that this tension surrounding audience participation was resolved, I would argue, this example is illustrative once again of the paradox of liveness. It attests to a need among producers to manage television so that it remains attractive for viewers according to their intentions, rather than allowing viewers to create potentially unwatchable television (or television that is too niche-oriented). Television producers feel they need to balance making "good" television with offering audiences participatory experiences (which they are thought to desire).

The Future of Broadcast TV

The two tensions discussed above help us consider the standing of broadcast television within the present media landscape, and particularly of social TV as a strategy. The suggestion that digital platforms would result in the end of broadcasting has proved untenable—because episodic drama and event TV continue to attract what could be characterized as mass audiences, and also because digital platforms are being used to supplement television (Gray and Lotz 2012; Gillan 2011; Ytreberg 2009), helping to reassert the significance of the broadcast medium. This has been demonstrated through *The Voice*, particularly in terms of the support that digital platforms can offer liveness. We can convincingly conclude that the mass communication paradigm has not disappeared but has merely changed (Gripsrud 2010; Turner 2009).

For now, the business model of the networks continues to center on calculations that assume that audiences will watch television live, or on what Philip Napoli (2011) calls "exposure metrics." This explains the need to have people watch broadcast television live. However, the Nielsen Company, a key player in measuring television ratings, introduced "Twitter TV Ratings" in 2013, an industry metric that complements TV ratings with insights garnered from Twitter data. In 2016 it announced that this would be expanded to include Facebook activities around shows. The introduction of these metrics changes the value of social media platforms by tracking audience sentiment in real time. This development points to the revaluing of television audiences as the industry slowly shifts away from rationalizing audiences in terms of exposure metrics alone (Napoli 2011). These days, audience research is no longer just about televisions being switched on to particular programs, but also about other aspects of audience behavior and response, captured under the umbrella term "engagement." This suggests that for the industry, participatory television will play an increasingly large role in the future.

6
Social Media's New Relation to the Live

The feeds of platforms like Twitter and Facebook are examples of what is sometimes referred to as the "real-time web." "Real time" here stresses how content on these platforms is constantly being updated, in contrast to the "static web," which is organized around webpages and links (Weltevrede, Helmond, and Gerlitz 2014). "News Feed," the central feature on Facebook, is an example of the real-time web; as it happens, it is widely referred to as being "live." By analyzing Facebook and its News Feed, I can explore the emergence of a very different user relationship to liveness from what is offered by broadcast media. This producer relation, already latent on the Original Livestream platform, gives rise to several tensions surrounding the live.[79] These tensions arise here because, as Tarleton Gillespie (2015) has pointed out, the "stuff" on social media platforms isn't the product of mere user participation; the platforms themselves also "pick and choose." In other words, they intervene in what users do—through not just the logic of their algorithms but also the imperatives of their business model and their enforcement of community guidelines.

In the previous chapter, I used liveness as a means to analyze the standoff between broadcast media and social media as manifested in a series of tensions surrounding the live. This chapter picks up again on the interrelation between broadcast media and social media. However, it should be recognized here that Facebook is a particularly challenging subject to research. Not only is it a moving target—constantly "under construction"—but due to its convergence with many other websites and platforms it also has no real contours: its reach seems to be ever expanding across the Web. My research primarily considers the platform in its manifestation during the period spanning November and December 2012. That the platform is persistently updated and that therefore many of its features have since been altered do not invalidate the insights that Facebook can generate with reference to liveness.[80]

The Facebook Metatext: Me and My Friends

To introduce Facebook and review its metatext, I use information gathered on the platform itself, from official Facebook blog entries, and from comments from an interview with Facebook's founder and CEO, Mark Zuckerberg. I also use academic reflections on the identity of Facebook (Gehl 2013; van Dijck 2013b), which paint a clear picture of Facebook's self-presentation as a platform for mediating social relations. In addition, these texts inform my dealings with the metatext surrounding the News Feed and its various "Live Feed" incarnations.

Like other social networking sites, Facebook offers users a platform to maintain social relations online. Use of Facebook at the outset is rather simple: after registration, users receive their own "Timeline" (profile page) and can "friend" other users, which means "subscribing" to their posts. They can also join groups or "like" celebrities, products, and companies.

Social networking sites (SNS) such as Facebook are not a new phenomenon. As early as 1995, a website named Classmates.com fulfilled a similar function (Scholz 2008). Zuckerberg launched Facebook in 2004 under the name "The Facebook"; originally, it targeted Harvard University students and academic staff. Membership was later extended to various educational institutions, and the site then introduced "networks" (made up of peers from high school, or of regional and corporate contacts), requiring that users be part of such a network in order to sign up. However, as the site's user base expanded, it turned out that the network idea did not scale well (boyd and Hargittai 2010), and so, in September 2006, Facebook was opened to the public.

Around the time that I was studying the Facebook platform back in 2012 it had 955 million monthly active users and 552 million daily active users (Taylor 2012). In November of that year, the official Facebook homepage stated that its mission was "to give people the power to share and make the world more open and connected." Like other social networking sites, Jenny Kennedy (Kennedy 2013) notes, Facebook deploys a "sharing" rhetoric that establishes its function as a social facilitator and promotes ideas of togetherness. If a sharing rhetoric is common to social media platforms in general, Facebook positions itself as an intermediary in personal relationships in particular. Or as they put it themselves, "Facebook helps you connect and share with the people in your life." Aside from its slogan, this orientation is evident in the term it uses to describe the connections people make on the platform: "friends" rather than "contacts" (LinkedIn) or "followers" (Twitter and Instagram).

How users are invited to post to the platform is another telling indication of how Facebook positions itself. What a user posts through a "Status Update" appears on his or her Timeline (personal page) but is also filtered and possibly presented in friends' News Feeds (found on their front page). The text used to prompt posts in this field had been "[user id] is." This formulation, however, invited grammatically awkward sentences from users who felt "forced" into writing about themselves in the third person (Schiffman 2007), and it was dropped in late 2007. In 2009, the prompting text in the Status Update function was modified again. Whereas the original text encouraged users to post via the question "What are you doing right now?" from this point on they were asked, "What's on your mind?" Later in 2011, the two subquestions "Who are you with?" and "Where are you?" were appended to this text.

These tweaks to the Status Update show how the platform consistently invited users to share about *themselves*: what they were thinking about or doing and/or where they were hanging out, and with whom. The idea of the platform being about the users corresponds also to how boyd (2008) typifies social networking sites: as being about "me and my friends."

In a 2010 interview with *Time* magazine, Zuckerberg remarked:

> The thing that I really care about is making the world more open and connected.... Open means having access to more information, right? More transparency, being able to share things and have a voice in the world. And connected is helping people stay in touch and maintain empathy for each other, and bandwidth. (qtd. in Grossman 2010, n.p.)

The values of openness and connectedness, stressed by Zuckerberg in this interview, are perpetuated throughout Facebook's self-presentation—in official statements and in how the platform encourages users to share through its interface. Facebook's language, as Robert W. Gehl (2013) has pointed out, also contains many metaphors of citizenship and democracy. The idea of the platform as some kind of a nation-state materialized most clearly in 2009, when the first Facebook Site Governance vote took place. The company even maintains that its daily generation of user data contributes to democracy and is vital for social connection (Gehl 2013).

The Space of Participation

In its metatext, Facebook makes strong claims about sharing and sociality—claims that have been reproduced in popular discourse. In what follows, I discuss those features of the platform that are relevant to a basic understanding of its space of participation.[81] I seek to clarify here which relations are being mediated on the platform, and how.

After logging in on Facebook, the 2012 user was directed to a homepage. The News Feed feature, found in the center column, was basically an aggregation of posts from people in a user's social network. This aggregation, which I cover below in greater detail, was filtered through the EdgeRank algorithm. In being so central to the platform, the feature made Facebook a platform primarily about sharing things with friends.

Above the News Feed was a Status Update field. The upper toolbar had three simple icons next to a search toolbar: "Friend Requests" (two silhouettes), "Messages" (a text bubble), and "Notifications" (a globe). On the other side of the search toolbar was a profile image with one's username, which functioned as a link to one's profile page ("Timeline"), along with a "Find Friends" button and a dropdown "Home" menu (with options to "Advertise on Facebook," go to one's "Account Settings" or "Privacy Settings," log out, or consult a "Help" module).

The left column on the homepage featured several options below a thumbnail of the user's profile picture (with the thumbnail linking to his or her Timeline): "News Feed," "Messages," "Events," and "Find Friends" (from top to bottom).[82] The right column on the homepage, at the top, listed birthdays and upcoming events; below that was a section with "Sponsored links" and links to Facebook-related settings such as "Cookies," "Privacy," and a language-setting option. Next to the right column was the "Ticker" feature, stretching from top to bottom, with a little box at the bottom for the Chat feature.

The Facebook platform offered several ways for users to interact with one another. They could post their current status, share photos/videos, or ask a question through the Status Update feature on the homepage (previously discussed in terms of its address to the user). They could "like" or "comment" on the platform activities of others in their social network, or post directly on their Timelines; they could also message other users through the embedded messaging feature, or chat with them via the Chat feature.

This brief account of the platform interface at the time highlights again the various aspects of the platform's social identity as proposed by the metatext. It should be pointed out, however, that while Facebook was positioned as a social platform, not all forms of social interaction afforded here were centered on real-time communication, let alone addressed as being "live." In line with the aims of this book, the focus here is on how liveness was constructed on the platform. To maintain this focus, I explore how the platform itself co-constructed liveness, rather than on how third parties did this through their use of the platform (e.g., by hosting "virtual viewing parties" around TV shows and event television).

I have omitted any consideration of the Facebook Chat feature in this chapter, which may seem puzzling, but I have a good reason for ignoring it—a reason that ties in with insights from chapter 3 on the platform Livestream. Although a chat feature taps into values of both real time and sociality, it is not referred to as being "live" in either the metatext or the user responses. The most plausible explanation for this is that the function facilitates one-to-one interaction, with only limited intervention on the part of Facebook (unlike its other social tools, such as the News Feed). However, when a celebrity takes part in an organized chat session through the platform, these customarily unmediated streams become orchestrated and monitored—and the sessions are heavily promoted as being "live." Here too, then, the relation between liveness and institutionalization is highlighted.

Aside from the platform's design, its business imperatives also inform its organization of social interaction. Over the course of several financing rounds, Facebook has found investors in the likes of Digital Sky Technologies, Li Ka-shing, Goldman Sachs, and the venture capital firms Elevation Partners, Accel Partners, Meritech Capital Partners, and Greylock Partners (Mangalindan 2011). The most publicized business transaction involving Facebook was perhaps Microsoft's 2007 purchase of a 1.7 percent stake in the social network for $240 million (Stone 2007). In May 2012, the company's first initial public offering (IPO) was held, capitalizing $104 billion. On the implications of the IPO, an analyst at Robert W. Baird & Company stated:

> Before they were a public company, Facebook was judged by growth in users.... Now that they are so well penetrated in most Western markets, growth has to translate into monetization. (qtd. in Sengupta 2012)

Social media companies face something of a quandary after their early successes have (prematurely) been heralded. Despite their awesome capabilities for building audiences—which sparked the initial euphoria—developing the right business model has proven extremely challenging for them. For instance, established in 2006, Twitter's business model after ten years remains "broken," in that the company faces negative profits that continue to worsen over time (Trainer 2016).

Facebook has a mix of strategies for monetization, although it focuses strongly on targeting users on the basis of their personal data. Lev Grossman, writing in a 2010 profile of Zuckerberg for *Time*, put the matter more bluntly:

> Facebook has a dual identity, as both a for-profit business and a medium for our personal lives, and those two identities don't always sit comfortably side by side. (Grossman 2010)

The friction between these two Facebook identities has also been addressed by José van Dijck, among others. She writes,

> Facebook's business model is…a contentious balancing act between stimulating users' activity and exploiting it; its success ultimately depends on customers' willingness to contribute data and to allow maximum data mining. (van Dijck 2013a, 64)

Facebook sells customized metadata for targeted marketing in the Sponsored banner; in addition, it features "Sponsored Stories" in the News Feed. Users also have the opportunity to purchase Facebook Gifts, and the platform offers integrated paid services such as social games. In the meantime, it continues to experiment with new revenue streams.

In 2012, for instance, Facebook tested a promoted-post system, allowing users to pay to bump their status updates higher in the News Feed (Hill 2012). The "regime of visibility" inherent to the logic of the News Feed, it has been argued, creates a desire to participate by threatening those who do not with invisibility (Bucher 2012). Participation, however, comes at a cost. As Navneet Alang has pointed out in TECHi:

> What [Zuckerberg] failed to mention was that the more you participate in this 'openness and connection,' the more you contribute to Facebook's main revenue stream. (2010, n.p.)

Alang, furthermore, comments on how it is not in the interest of Facebook to allow users more privacy (or to give them more fine-grained privacy settings), because its business model thrives on personalized advertisements. Generic ads are less lucrative for the company, so the platform aims to collect as much data about its users as it can so as to offer advertisers the prospect of highly targeted, individualized ads.

The financial success of Facebook—free to join, and not profitable until 2009—ultimately relies on users sharing content (e.g., short messages, photos/videos, or files) and, in the process, generating data. Users do this in ways both obvious and hidden. By navigating the platform, and in liking and commenting on content, users generate data that is used for processes of which they are often not fully aware. Sharing on social media, then, no longer just concerns the content that users post and browse through but also, increasingly, automatically tracked behavioral information (Lampinen 2015). User activity is channeled by design to improve the underlying information systems—and by complying with what the design suggests, users are involved in what has been called "implicit participation" (Schäfer 2011).

Facebook encourages user interaction through its user address. The most basic example of this means of interaction in the 2012 interface is the prompt text in Status Update. Also, when users had a pending friend request or received a message and/or a notification of activities relating to their profile, the icons on their homepage would not only turn from dark blue to light blue, but in the upper right-hand corner of the icon space, a red square with a number would also emerge. This number specified the actions that needed attending to. When clicked on, a list of items was loaded and the red square disappeared. There are other examples as well, including the incentive to recommend friends to newcomers, or the aggregation of comments as some sort of a "birthday feed" within the News Feed, making birthdays more visible and encouraging others to congratulate the birthday boy or girl.

Legal forces also shape activity on Facebook. In registering with the site, a user has to agree to its Terms of Service (ToS), which specify user rights and responsibilities. A simple but strong example of its guidelines (or, if you like, restrictions) is that users are not allowed to misrepresent themselves on Facebook or use a false name. Users violating this policy risk having their accounts terminated. In 2014, for instance, Facebook enforced its policy and deleted several hundred profiles of drag queens and transgender people for violating its real-name policy. Shortly afterward, following public outrage over the expulsions, they apologized and changed the policy. These changes were specifically directed at establishing "more awareness of context of real-name complaints" (Hern 2015).

Although people don't pay to use Facebook, they sign away their rights to the content they upload and they consent to being monitored. The company can also share the data that are collected about their interactions with third parties. Some academics (Andrejevic 2008; Fuchs 2011; Palmer 2003; Petersen 2008; Scholz 2008; Terranova 2004) see this as a form of exploitation, as user data is ultimately commodified in the process (Petersen 2008).

That data plays a central role in the operations of Facebook is evident from its Data Use Policy. Here, the platform offers some general claims about how it uses the data it amasses:

> We use the information we receive about you in connection with the services and features we provide to you and other users like your friends, our partners, the advertisers that purchase ads on the site, and the developers that build the games, applications, and websites you use.

Data are collected not only about users' own preferences and connections on Facebook, but also beyond its confines, as services across the Web are connected to the social graph and provide input about the experience of the site. The concept of the social graph was introduced by Facebook and concerns the idea of mapping out "all the connections between people and the things they care about" (Hicks 2010). While laws prescribe how data can be implemented for specific purposes, the legal system has yet to catch up with the state of affairs pertaining to many of the practices described here.

In light of legal issues, Facebook has faced considerable public backlash, specifically over its privacy policies (or lack of clear privacy assurances). Time and time again the introduction of new privacy policies has resulted in users forming protest groups (Fletcher 2010). In fact, the platform is in constant negotiation with its users over privacy.

The Live Feeds of the News Feed

The imperatives of Facebook's business model, its terms of use, and the adaptive algorithmic architectures operating below the surface of its interface determine how connections on Facebook are curated and displayed (Bucher 2015). When the News Feed feature was introduced, it transformed Facebook "from a network of connected Web pages into a personalized newspaper featuring (and created by) [one's] friends" (Pariser 2012, 37). The Facebook homepage, to which users are directed when logging on to the site, centers on this feature. It offers users a personalized list of news stories, based on their online activities. Although Facebook isn't itself understood as "live," this particular feature is associated with liveness, both in popular discourse and by the platform itself.

The News Feed was launched on September 6, 2006, and was introduced as a tool to highlight what was happening in one's social circle. Its rationale was explained to the world on *The Facebook Blog* as follows:

> It updates a personalized list of news stories throughout the day, so you'll know when Mark adds Britney Spears to his Favorites or when your crush is single again. Now, whenever you log in, you'll get the latest headlines generated by the activity of your friends and social groups. (Sanghvi 2006, n.p.)

The tool helps to manage all of the users' Facebook connections, and allows them to stay more up-to-date on the lives of their friends. Earlier in this chapter, I pointed out that by sharing through the Status Update feature, a user posts directly to his or her own "Timeline," and that his or her activity is (selectively) shared with friends through the News Feed. These friends can "like" or comment on these shared statuses, photos, videos, or links, either directly on a given friend's (or one's own) Timeline or through the News Feed.

Since 2006, the News Feed has undergone numerous revisions. By exploring the development of the feature, I aim to trace how its liveness has been refashioned over time. To do so, I analyze the "Live Feed," "Most Recent," and "Ticker" features, each of which can be associated with a particular articulation of the live. Throughout this exploration, I target both the specific metatext related to the feature (which does indeed reflect on its liveness), sourced primarily from Facebook's interface and the Facebook blog, and the particular affordances of the different feeds that make up the feature. Of course, this approach cannot lead to an exhaustive consideration of the changes made to the feature, but it does allow me to reflect on how the live has been refashioned over time.

Live Feed

On October 23, 2009, Facebook introduced the Live Feed (Dybwad 2009), a view within the News Feed that users could switch to by clicking a tab (see figure 6). In contrast to the default News Feed view, which singled out the most "interesting" things that had happened in the past day, the Live Feed, as its name suggested, revolved around seeing what was happening right now. As a post on *The Facebook Blog* explained: "As long as you remain logged into Facebook, you'll continue to see posts and activity from your friends in real-time" (Yung 2009, n.p.)

Contrary to popular belief, the Live Feed was not a neutral stream that aggregated friends' activities as they were posted. For Facebook users with more than 250 connections, selection figured in to govern how the Live Feed operated. In part, the method of selection was based on a calculated sense of relevance, to a specific user, of these connections and their posts. This was clarified in the News Feed options, where Facebook stated the following:

> Live Feed automatically determines which friends to include based on who Facebook thinks you want to hear from most. You can manually adjust this list below.

What the user saw, in other words, was a result of inferences made on the basis of their own user behavior and that of their

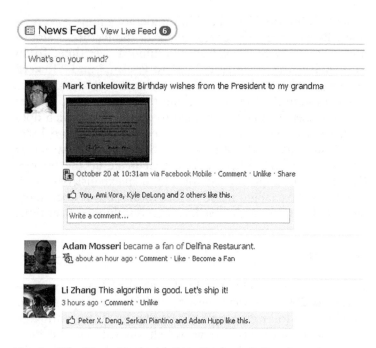

Fig. 6:   The News Feed with Live Feed tab (taken from a Facebook blog entry [Yung 2009])

friends. The user could exercise some influence over how these connections weighed into the feed by selecting "Show More" or "Hide" when hovering over a friend's post.

Most Recent

In early 2010, Facebook rolled out a new homepage design. The two News Feed streams were renamed. There was now a "Top News" view, which offered a summary of top stories, and a "Most Recent" view, described in a Facebook blog post as "a live feed of all stories" (Quintana 2010, n.p.). This system was developed in order to cater to infrequent Facebook users; for them, Top News was featured as their home page's default view. The idea was that providing top stories would help these users catch up on activities that had

happened while they had been away (which a mere aggregation of the most recent posts could not do).

Top News was based on an algorithm that determined the
purported relevance of postings to a particular user. This
estimate of relevance was calculated in part through the user's
earlier interactions with the platform, and in part by type of
content. It stood in contrast to the chronological list provided
by the Most Recent feed, which Facebook claimed delivered
a view of "all updates from your friends" (Quintana 2010).
In Top News, which featured highlights, time decay was less
of an issue. The Most Recent feed, in its being organized
according to chronology and contrasted to a feed organized
by relevance, is very similar to—if not simply the rebranding
of—the Live Feed.

Ticker

In late September 2011, the News Feed was changed from
a feature that offered the choice between two views to a
single feed that showed Top News high up in the feed, with
Recent Stories further below. Facebook claimed to have made
this change to cater to frequent and infrequent Facebook
users alike. In *The Facebook Blog* posting announcing the
changes, an analogy was made between the News Feed and
a newspaper:

> When you pick up a newspaper after not reading it for a week,
> the front page quickly clues you into the most interesting
> stories. In the past, News Feed hasn't worked like that.
> Updates slide down in chronological order so it's tough to
> zero in on what matters most. Now, News Feed will act more
> like your own personal newspaper. (Tonkelowitz 2011, n.p.)

Henceforth, all stories were featured in a single stream, with
the top stories on top, marked with a blue corner, and the
more recent stories appearing below in chronological order.

Aside from merging Top News and Most Recent into a
single feed, with top stories marked with a blue corner, the
platform also introduced another feed made up of real-time
posts, named Ticker. It was a real-time rolling list of one's
friends' activities featured in the right margin as the user

navigated the platform. As noted on *The Facebook Blog*, Ticker required a steady flow of content to be useful and was therefore available only to users with "enough" platform activity.

In both official Facebook blog posts and popular discourse, Ticker has been referred to as "the live ticker," which warrants its inclusion in this study. It is connected to Facebook's Open Graph protocol, which I explain a bit more in the next section. The Facebook Help Center has explained the difference between Ticker and the central News Feed as follows:

> Ticker, on the right-hand side of your account, lets you see all your friends' activity in real-time. When you hover over an item in ticker, you can see the full story and join the conversation as it happens. Ticker updates itself as as [*sic*] stories happen. This gives you a more complete picture of what your friends are doing, right now.

If a user has been idle on Facebook for more than fifteen minutes, Ticker stops updating. And in contrast to the Most Recent feed, which comprises rich media updates, it is a text-only feed. According to the Facebook FAQ:

> Ticker includes live stories—things like status updates, friendships, photos, videos, links, likes and comments. You can see this activity elsewhere on Facebook. Ticker just lets you see it as it happens.

Tonkelowitz explains the specific advantage of Ticker over the content brought through the News Feed:

> Ticker shows you the same stuff you were already seeing on Facebook, but it brings your conversations to life by displaying updates instantaneously. Now when a friend comments, asks a question or shares something like a check in, you'll be able to join the conversation right away. (2011, n.p.)

The blog entry that introduced Ticker to users places a strong emphasis on the "right now" quality of the feature. Because aggregating and updating stories occur in real time, it suggests, it enables users to participate in ongoing activities.

The Algorithms of the News Feed

The discussion of the different incarnations of the "live" feeds in Facebook's News Feed has shown that each is contrasted to another feed that is the product of the "work" of certain algorithms. The two central Facebook algorithms are EdgeRank and GraphRank.

EdgeRank governs what is displayed in the News Feed, and how high up specific postings make it in the feed. It is said to construct a "regime of visibility" on Facebook (Bucher 2012). Because algorithms are the "secret sauce" of companies these days, a complete breakdown of the Facebook algorithms here is impossible (quite apart from the fact that they are continually tweaked). My interest in the live, however, does not demand in-depth knowledge of their every technical detail; an understanding of their basic operating principles is sufficient to engage with them on a theoretical level.[83]

In 2010, Facebook engineers Ruchi Sanghvi and Ari Steinberg gave Jason Kincaid of *TechCrunch* a rundown of the factors involved in the making of EdgeRank's calculations. They explained that each item appearing in the News Feed is called an "Object." An Object that another user interacts with, for instance by tagging or commenting on it, is called an "Edge." And an Edge, they pointed out, has three components important to the Edgerank algorithm. These are:

u.—The affinity score between viewing user and Edge creator
w.—The weight for this Edge type (create, comment, like, tag, etc.)
d.—The time decay factor, based on how long ago the Edge was created. (Kincaid 2010, n.p.)

The affinity score is determined by calculating the number of interactions between two Facebook members. A friend that is often interacted with (directly or indirectly) has a higher affinity score for a particular user than a friend whose profile page one hardly visits and whose objects one rarely responds to. How the weight of an Edge type is determined is not entirely clear, but certain Edges are more important than others (and are thus given more weight). Kincaid speculates, for example, that a Comment is valued more than a Like. The third factor involves time, or more precisely immediacy: an Object is deemed more relevant the newer it is. Multiplying the factors of all the Edges and adding their scores up create an Object's EdgeRank. The value of this ranking determines whether the Object makes it into the feed (the higher the number, the more likely this is).

In September 2011 Facebook introduced GraphRank, the algorithm responsible for distributing Open Graph application activity across the News Feed, Ticker, and Timeline. It does not deal with page posts or status updates, but rather finds apps that are popular with a Facebook users' friends. Together, EdgeRank and GraphRank personalize Facebook for its users.

Returning, then, to the specific question of the live in the News Feed, we see a crucial condition of liveness as outlined in chapter 5. Namely, each of the live feed manifestations (e.g., Live Feed, Most Recent, and Ticker) emerged in contrast to a non-live counterpart. The meaning of the Live Feed was established through a contrast with the output of the EdgeRank algorithms that filtered the News Feed. Later, the Most Recent feed organized stories chronologically rather than around relevance, and with substantially less filtering than had been the case with Top News. Then, with Ticker as the live feed, liveness was no longer only about the filtering process, but also about real-time updating—about allowing users to participate in the ongoing activities of their connections. These three articulations of a "live feed" illustrate the flexibility of the term "live" as its point of reference (as revealed by the noun it is combined with, or its context); we can see how its meaning has changed over time.

In considering these constructions of liveness, it is key to consider that Facebook's infrastructure is privately owned and operated. The platform exerts significant influence, specifically through design, over how people represent themselves and maintain relations with others online. In this particular configuration, numerous actors shape these relations—but the underlying algorithms also play a particularly important role (not least because what they are doing is not always evident or traceable).

User Responses: Privacy Issues

In an attempt to understand how users give meaning to the platform, I now move on and reflect on platform use, and consider how user practices relate to the platform's framing by the metatext. I also consider recurring user discussions of privacy, coinciding with changes in the operation of the platform. Both these points are indicative of the producer relation to liveness that I mentioned in the introduction to this chapter.

In considering platform use, it is helpful to briefly contextualize Facebook's popularity at the time of the research. In 2012, Facebook's population penetration was 30.25 percent in Europe and 45.55 percent in North America (Erickson 2012).[84] Because of its large-scale adoption, the media industry has become interested in how the platform has changed media consumption habits. In 2011, Pew Research reported that 52 percent of users in the United States visited the website daily, and 32 percent one to five days a week (Lenhart et al. 2011).

Zeroing in on how Facebook is being used, another Pew Research study found that on an average day:

15% of Facebook users update their own status
22% comment on another's post or status
20% comment on another user's photos
26% 'like' another user's content
10% send another user a private message. (Hampton et al. 2011)

Whereas these percentages indicate how users interact on Facebook around content and with others, it does not reveal what type of content is being shared and interacted with. For Facebook, as mentioned, it is desirable that users share often, because doing so enables the company to collect information about them, both to sell it to third parties and to stimulate interactions on the platform. For users, the making of many connections is attractive because it enables them to acquire social capital (Ellison, Steinfeld, and Lampe in van Dijck 2013a, 47). Sharing, in turn, is what keeps the News Feed alive. Without a constant stream of content, a user's feed flatlines, and being on Facebook becomes uninteresting.

In an attempt to establish what people share on the site, I examined the "Wall" for each of twenty-five randomly selected Facebook friends of my own.[85] Of these friends, two had their Wall feature disabled. Taking September 1, 2011, as my point of reference, I looked at the last ten Objects the users themselves shared on their Walls, collecting 230 contributions in total. These contributions are admittedly biased in that they reflect my social circle. But even though they do not constitute a representative selection of Objects, the items I examined can give us an idea of how the platform was used and, by extension, understood by its users—thus providing a useful complement to ideas expressed through the metatext.

Of the 230 contributions, 132 were either comments on what the users had just been doing, were doing, or intended to do, or were thoughts and opinions that were not explicitly related to something that had recently taken place or was about to take place. Only four contributions were links to news stories. The remaining 94 were shares of photos or videos, check-ins, and links to websites that were not news-related. Such use suggests that users understood the platform primarily as a space to share personal information.

This may, of course, seem unsurprising, because this use corresponds to how Facebook itself envisions the platform and ties in with its promise of direct access to the lives of one's friends. However, it is necessary to underline this con-clusion, especially in light of the debate about whether online social networks are replacing mainstream media outlets as sites for news consumption. Consider, in this context, claims that social media platforms such as Twitter and Facebook played a crucial role in spreading the news of the death of Osama Bin Laden.[86] The *Washington Post* and the Pew Research Center, after asking Americans how they first heard of the Bin Laden raid, countered such assessments by con-cluding that most people first heard the news through televi-sion (58 percent) rather than online (11 percent) ("Washington Post-Pew Research Center Poll" n.d.).[87] As stated in the origi-nal Pew report:

> Facebook and Twitter are now pathways to news, but their role may not be as large as some have suggested. The popula-tion that uses these networks for news at all is still relatively

small, especially the part that does so very often. (Mitchell, Rosenstiel, and Christian 2012, n.p.)

How Facebook is promoted and used supports the idea that the platform is about connecting people to one another, and only in this role does it also become a space for the exchange of news. This idea of connecting people is therefore not just a rhetorical claim pushed at users through the metatext and inscribed in the platform's design, but is in fact underscored by people's actual Facebook use (at least in 2010).

In 2010 the websites of major media institutions were still the preferred destination for online news consumption, as opposed to social media platforms and the sites of internet-based organizations (Baumgartner and Morris 2010). The landscape has been changing as the influence of social media on news consumption is increasing. The Pew Research Center reported that in 2013, 30 percent of U.S. adults use Facebook to keep up with news (Matsa and Mitchell 2014). Moreover, Facebook has since launched an Instant Articles program, allowing media outlets to distribute interactive articles for the mobile app that load faster. As explained by Michael Reckhow (2015), a product manager at Facebook, "Publishers can sell ads in their articles and keep the revenue, or they can choose to use Facebook's Audience Network to monetize unsold inventory" (n.p.). Facebook is thus working hard at becoming a destination platform for news about the "world" as well (rather than just the individual). It furthermore suggests that the relationship between social media and the mainstream media are not necessarily one of competition.

Having discussed what user practices imply about their understanding of Facebook, I now move to discuss what users *say* about the platform, and specifically its liveness. Because of the many public debates the platform has provoked, I zoom in here on the tendency to reflect about issues of privacy, as has been reported by the press and in academic publications. The reason for this is that discontent about privacy on Facebook highlights a tension surrounding the live, centering on the fact that on the sort of platforms discussed here, users themselves are what liveness promises direct access to. In the process, inevitably, user information is made highly visible to others. The problem here is that shared information on Facebook concerns not just content that has consciously been put online, but also other information about users' online activities.

Whenever a new feature or update is introduced, indeed, Facebook is met with a new wave of public outcry, accompanied by legal debates over the implications this current iteration of the platform has for user privacy. The launch of the News Feed in 2006, for instance, created public uproar, as users felt they were being "tracked" by the minute. Consequently, they pushed for Facebook to introduce privacy tools to give users more control over how information was shared (boyd 2008). Zuckerberg has brushed off such incidents, putting the blame on users rather than Facebook. He stated that the company's role is to "[figure] out what the next things are that everyone wants to do and then [bring] them along to get them there" (qtd. in Fletcher 2010). The problem surrounding privacy, according to such claims, stems from Facebook having to "educate" users on the norms around sharing.

The introduction of the Ticker, too, was followed by public outrage over privacy issues, and the feature quickly acquired the nickname "creeper ticker" in online discussions (Constine 2013). Facebook, in reply to claims that the feature changed users' default privacy settings, argued that user activity had simply become more visible as it unfolded in real time. The introduction of the Ticker, indeed, marked a shift in strategy for the platform: from the rendering visible of deliberately shared content to the automatic sharing of user activities without explicit user consent (Gordhamer 2011). Many users experienced this making visible of "their" data, first by the News Feed and then by the Ticker, as an invasion of their privacy. At the time of the latter's release, it was unclear how they could prevent their activities from being shown in other people's Tickers—and this became a problem.

Tension Surrounding the Live: Producer Relation to Liveness

In relation to privacy issues on social media, danah boyd (2008) has argued that privacy is in fact not about having no one know what a user is doing, but rather about users being able to control and limit public knowledge of their activity. Such an interpretation of privacy rights, or at least norms, comes down to an understanding of privacy in terms of the users' capacity to control content flow. Public dissatisfaction with Facebook over privacy, indeed, has resulted from how platform changes have affected the way that users relate to platform content and to others.

Such dissatisfaction, I would contend, points once again to a tension surrounding the live. This tension arises because users now not only have a user relation to liveness, as is the case with traditional broadcast media, but also a producer relation to liveness. On Facebook, rather than merely consuming a stream of content, users also provide content and the data that drives the platform.[88] Overall, the relation between users and content is more dynamic than in the broadcast model, where content is simply pushed from a center to a periphery. The relation here is instead formed by the interactions among users, in combination with Facebook's underlying algorithms.

Such observations hark back to insights on the topic of broadcast flow. As early as 2004, William Uricchio (2004), looking at viewer-television interfaces, addressed a pattern of shifting agency—from television programmers to RCD-equipped viewers to metadata programmers and adaptive agent designers. With social media platforms, this trend has infiltrated media consumption at large, in that entertainment platforms (e.g., YouTube, Netflix) and retail platforms (e.g., Amazon) actually *steer* user consumption, their algorithms interacting with user data to create individualized flows of content. These insights into the changing role of users have been extended in a 2011 essay, also by Uricchio, who points to an important question raised by algorithmic intervention. His analysis of the image application Photosynth illustrates how authorship here has become problematic and multiple. In such applications, he explains, there are many actors: the people providing the content, those navigating the content, the authors of the algorithm, and finally the algorithm itself, which makes only certain content visible.

Uricchio's insight into how the algorithmic presence reworks subject-object relations, a means to draw attention to what the author calls "algorithmic intermediation," can be extended to numerous applications, including Facebook and Twitter. In these instances, also, there is not a central perspective through which one experiences the platform and its content—as would be the case in traditional television. Although Facebook is personalized for each user, people do share social circles in common, and in this manner the platform can make shared friends into a topical resource for conversation. This shared frame of reference is, in fact, what the News Feed helps to achieve.

However, with users as the locus of liveness in the feed, a tension arises between the promise of direct access to others' lives, and the feeling among those users—also the subjects of the liveness of social media—that their privacy is being invaded. The producer relation to liveness, which this tension results from, has various implications. In what follows, I explore each of these implications in turn, connecting them to current debates in media studies. The three points I raise are closely connected and help me to tease out how content is managed on a social media platform such as Facebook.

Between Sticky and Spreadable Media

I have argued throughout this chapter that users of social media, because they contribute the content that essentially drives these platforms, have both a user relation and a producer relation to liveness. Although platform design is highly influential as to how comments, links, videos, and photos are shared (which makes the promise of liveness effectively a promise to delimit users' control), what is being shared, for the most part, and notwithstanding some techno-cultural and legal constraints, is up to the user. The emergence of social media platforms, in other words, has redefined the relation between media industries and users. This redefinition, in turn, strikes at the core of a tension surrounding the live.

As a form of audience participation, user sharing has attracted academic attention with the publication of *Spreadable Media* (2013). In this book, Henry Jenkins, Sam Ford, and Joshua Green investigate how media content is spread across cultures through what they see as a mix of top-down and bottom-up forces. Rather than looking at the reception and production practices of audiences, which have been the focus of research on participatory culture thus far, they investigate online media circulation. They address the limitations of the current "stickiness model," wherein web traffic defines online success. As they explain,

> The use of 'stickiness' in the business setting refers to centralizing the audience's presence in a particular online location to generate advertising revenue or sales. (Jenkins, Ford, and Green 2013, 4)

Stickiness, then, harks back to the broadcast media era and its most characteristic business model. "Spreadability," on the other hand, concerns how media content circulates within a networked culture (rather than how attention is aggregated centrally). Jenkins et al. argue that the media industry should encourage access to content from multiple sites and allow users to engage with content in their own ways: "The 'distribution' reach of sticky destinations and the 'circulation' reach of spreadable media should coexist" (Jenkins, Ford, and Green 2013, 8).

Jenkins et al. provide several examples in which the success of mainstream commercial media productions has not been driven by broadcast distribution, but has gained traction through its circulation on online networks. Susan Boyle's audition on *Britain's Got Talent* in 2009 is perhaps the best known of these instances and best illustrates the point they are making. Although the show was broadcast on television only in the UK, the clip of her audition was uploaded and shared on platforms such as YouTube and Facebook, bringing her to an international stage. The video attracted many more "eyeballs" online than through the original telecast.

Couldry's reflections on the relation between SNS and mainstream media resemble the idea of spreadable media:

> Far from SNS focusing an alternative 'centre,' the centring processes of SNS and mainstream media may well become increasingly intertwined like the strands of a double helix in a world where marketing itself strives increasingly to be like 'conversation' and to 'mobilize consumer agency'. (2012, 23–24)

As previously established, both *The Voice* and Facebook have hinted at such a double helix. In the former, the show stimulated conversation around airings, extending its reach on Twitter and other social platforms as viewers shared their thoughts and reactions with their online followers/friends. Moreover, *The Voice* made use of its official accounts on platforms such as YouTube, Twitter, Instagram, and Facebook. Returning to the case at hand, Facebook's use shows that people circulate content from the mainstream media (e.g., photos and videos) and link to news websites—albeit, in the period the analysis covered, not predominantly.

In interacting with the platform, and thereby circulating content and creating data, users at times feel their privacy is being threatened. They are not always aware of what data is being shared or how to specify who can see what they decide to share. The user is the topic of the News Feed and their lives are what the platform provides access to.

From Normative Frameworks to Statistical Ensembles

But aside from user-generated content, these platforms also collect and process user-generated data (for these notions, see Andrejevic 2009). The latter result from a fairly unconscious form of "participation" on the part of the user. The tension surrounding the live identified above draws attention to how the relations among users, and between users and the platform, are constructed with the help of algorithms processing user-generated data on the back end of the platform. Such processing penetrates all aspects of social life, and its role has obvious political and social ramifications (Willson 2014). In the future, then, the study of code and algorithms (e.g., in relation to how people use search engines, browsers, and applications as filtering mechanisms to navigate online information) is going to be ever more pertinent. In the context of this chapter, it is key primarily in considering the network within which algorithms operate, in order to reveal the roles and relations assumed by various actors.

Online users generate both content and data, and social media companies use both to create custom-tailored feeds and recommendations. The strategic use of personalized filters is based on the view that the more relevant material offered by a platform such as Facebook, the more advertisements that platform can sell, as advertisers will seek out the greater efficiency of personalized advertisements (or, in the case of Amazon, it is likely to sell more products through targeted recommendations). Eli Pariser (2012) fears that personalization, by eliminating chance encounters, will stifle personal growth and development, as people get stuck in what he calls an endless "you-loop." What users have clicked on in the past determines what they get to see in the future. He makes note of three specific issues that emerge in relation to this "filter bubble":

1. it pulls people apart, as they no longer share a frame of reference;
2. it is invisible, in the sense that users do not know the assumptions being made about them;
3. unlike with traditional media, where people select which filter to apply, having some knowledge of editors' bias, with the filter bubble people are unaware of these filters. (Pariser 2012, 9–10)

Within the Facebook News Feed, the different incarnations of the live feed have promised direct access to one's circle of "friends." The implicit reference point, here, was the filtering mechanisms working at the back-end of the platform for the Most Recent and Top Stories versions of the feed. Following a set of instructions, Facebook algorithms calculate what content is likely to be most "relevant" for a user out of all available content.

Search engines such as Google, Alexander Halavais proposes, create a topology of the Web, rather than making Web space "flat" (in Couldry 2012). Algorithms, here, seem to fulfill a similar function as the "editorial strategy" of mass media, in that they help select, juxtapose, and promote content within a single stream (van Dijck and Poell 2013). There are, however, important distinctions—not least in terms of how users themselves are involved and can steer information flows through their interaction. As Rieder and Sire rightly point out,

In the context of 'big data,' information is not managed through the conceptual and normative frameworks of journalistic practice or political deliberation but in terms of statistical ensembles, network centralities and frequencies of every kind (words, views, clicks, links, etc.). We simply cannot approach a search engine with the same critical toolset as we would use for, say, Fox News. (2014, 5)

The differences between the types of sorting on the web that result from the work of algorithms, and that which is a function of editorial decisions made by the mass media, reinforces once again the call for code literacy (Rushkoff 2011).

It must be recognized, of course, that users do have some control over what makes it into a News Feed (if only because they can select which friends to make part of their network). In 2012, when hovering over the top right-hand corner of an Object in the News Feed field, one would produce a button that offered a dropdown menu. Here users could opt to "Follow Post," "Hide [name of friend]," or "Report Story or Spam." Hiding users changed the frequency of the updates one got from a particular user and the type of updates. Furthermore, friends could be added to an "Acquaintance List," to make sure they hardly showed up in the News Feed at all. But these are all options with fairly limited consequences for the composition of the feed, in effect quite similar to the ability to toggle between the Top News and Most Recent feeds.

Moreover, the filtering done on platforms depends not just on platform activity and the work of algorithms but also on the choices that are made in, or the rationale behind, devising those algorithms. Willson (2014), discussing the politics of filtering, makes a distinction between two levels in this process that are potentially problematic. In doing so, she draws attention to the fact that the mere use of filtering software is already politically charged. She writes:

There is...an obvious difference in emphasis that can be made between some of the political implications as *a result or outcome of the filtering* done by SNSs and *the politics of the filtering* itself. The former partly depend upon the uses to which the data collection, for example, is put or the breadth of information that is excluded or included in any filtering process. The latter has to do more with the politics that are encoded and enacted in the technologies of filtering (as a practice and as a form) themselves. (Willson 2014, 12, original emphasis)

Both levels are important to consider: we should pay attention not only to which data are crunched and what is done with them, but also to the practice itself and the values that inform it. Filtering determines which kinds of information get distributed to users, and how it gets to them. Thus filtering is directly linked to the question of user privacy (i.e., what information about a user is acceptable to be shared with others) and their media consumption.

The Emerging "Like Economy"

Looking at the back end of Facebook makes visible how the platform attempts to extend capacities for data collection across the Web in what Gerlitz and Helmond (2013) call the emerging "Like economy." This economy is connected to the producer relation to liveness and to questions of privacy in particular, in that it influences how user data are handled. The Like economy has been defined thus:

> An infrastructure that allows the exchange of data, traffic, affects, connections and of course money, mediated through Social Plugins and most notably the Like button. (Gerlitz and Helmond 2013, 6)

They explain that whereas in the "link economy" of the informational web, established earlier, search engines such as Google relied on expert links made by webmasters and bloggers; on the social web, users now determine value by liking—and by extension, linking to—content on the web. In the Like economy, participation is not always a conscious act: "the underlying data mining processes foster participation by default, tracking users' browsing behaviour, storing Like button impressions or instantly sharing app engagement to the ticker" (Gerlitz and Helmond 2013, 14).

Particular to the economy of the social web is the connection of data collection to a platform's social graph. The connections mapped by the social graph, however, are no longer limited to connections between people, but have evolved to include objects (e.g., pages and photos) in the mapping of relations. Gerlitz and Helmond chart the presence of tracking devices on websites, and, in so doing, identify an alternative fabric of the web, based on associated trackers rather than the mutual linking between websites.[89] They suggest that from their sample of 1,000 global websites, about 18 percent of all websites feature Facebook Social Plugins and/or Facebook Connect. These plugins offer a way for the platform to complete its social graph on the basis of information generated across the Web. As Facebook CEO Mark Zuckerberg remarked upon introducing the Open Graph API at the F8 Software Developer conference in 2010: "These connections aren't just happening on Facebook, they're happening all over the Web, and today with the Open Graph we're bringing all these things together" (in Parr 2013). Social buttons thus facilitate this alternative web by supporting a decentralized form of data collection, while enabling data processing and capitalization to be recentralized on the platform.

The duality in the infrastructure that decentralizes data collection across the web and recentralizes its processing on a particular platform, thereby creating new centers of capital, alters the ways that people relate to and participate in media. This shift is evidence of how, in the gradual transition from the broadcast media to the social media era, media industries consider their audience to have started to change. As Couldry aptly explains,

> Their focus now is on the targeted search for individual high-value consumers not through specific media packages (programmes or series in which advertising can be placed) but via continuous online tracking which targets them *individually* and *continuously*, as they move around online. (Couldry 2012, 21)

The issues discussed in this chapter exemplify this transition particularly well. As a result of the strong role of user-collected data in the social media era, Schäfer's (2011) conceptual distinction between "implicit participation" and "explicit participation" (between the channeling of user activity through software design and conscious user decisions) becomes even more important to uphold when considering user agency. It offers a way to distinguish between what users more or less knowingly share and what they unknowingly share with others. With Ticker, for example, user-generated data *translates* to user-generated content, and user activities assumed to be private are made visible to various publics. Users become the locus of liveness—with consequences that some of them have experienced as a violation of their privacy. It should be apparent by now, however, that this is not a problem of technology alone, for it is equally the product of economic imperatives (the users must be encouraged to interact with the platform), legal necessities (e.g., Facebook's Terms and Data Use Policy), and cultural forces (i.e., what platform users deem socially acceptable).

Conclusions

Despite great scholarly interest in the concept "live," particularly in the realm of television studies, the various contributions to the debate have tended to zoom in on just one of the domains of liveness, thus limiting the scope of analysis. In part, this can be explained by the simple fact that most of these contributions are byproducts, rather than the primary focus, of particular academic discussions. The emergence of new forms of liveness in the social media era has highlighted the shortcomings of existing perspectives—which is why I have revisited the concept here. In an attempt to further our understanding of the category of the live, I have proposed analyzing liveness as a *constellation* which comprises the domains metatext, space of participation, and user responses. I have analyzed the constellation of liveness in four different cases: Livestream, eJamming, *The Voice*, and Facebook. Throughout these analyses I have harvested the dual benefit that comes with analyzing constellations of liveness. First, this analytic orientation has helped to develop an understanding of the *conditions* of liveness, and how the category operates within particular media configurations. And second, it has provided, in capturing how liveness is *mediated*, insight into the mechanisms through which media production, distribution, and consumption are managed. In these final pages, I want to reflect on the insights of the preceding chapters, and discuss how there is, in fact, much at stake with liveness.

The What, When, and How of Liveness

In this book, I have shown how the three domains involved in claims of liveness interact within different constellations to establish meaning and value for the "live." In each instance, the organization of relations among them differed significantly, as a result of each platform's specific configuration of techno-cultural, economic, and legal forces and the ways in which users interact with it. My working hypothesis has been that the *term* "live" is used only to describe media through which (symbolic) power is wielded/exercised. In other words, liveness seems to be activated only when particular (institutional) interests are being served. Facebook Chat, as pointed out in chapter 6, illustrates this circumstance particularly well. Although the feature is not referred to as being "live" by Facebook or its users, this changes as soon as celebrities are invited to chat with a community of fans; the event is then heavily promoted as being "live"—for only then is value ascribed to that which is being mediated. However—and this cannot be stressed enough—what is framed as "live" is not infinitely flexible. If liveness emerges, it does so as part of a continual interaction among the three domains.

The metatext frames how users interpret a platform's liveness and which values are being invoked in the process. User expectations are made most explicit when the platform fails to deliver on (its promise of) liveness, as seen in the case of eJamming. User responses prompted by this failure yielded several insights on the working of the concept. These largely revolved around the relations between liveness and, on the one hand, *real time*, which in this particular case created user expectations of online jamming without the experience of latency, and, on the other hand, *sociality*, which caused users to anticipate that they would be able to share their jamming sessions with an audience. The meaning and value of liveness on and around the eJamming platform were informed by conceptions from the offline music culture invoked in the metatext.

I have proposed also that an important paradox lies at the heart of liveness. This paradox has been explored, although not in the terms I have been using, by Paddy Scannell, most notably in his book *Television and the Meaning of 'Live'* (2014). Here Scannell drew attention to the invisible care structures in media that work hard to provide people with an authentic experience, which gives them a sense of communicative entitlement. In fact, each of the media (platforms) explored in this book, by invoking the live, promised its viewers/users an authentic, sociable experience, be it of a performance, an event, or interaction on their social network. Although everyone is given access to content simultaneously, individuals experience this content in their own ways and, through having experienced it, are granted the right to speak about it (Scannell 2001, 410). The paradox of liveness emerges from the contradiction between the hard work that goes into the production of the live and its seeming naturalness (rather than constructedness). In Scannell's account this hard work concerns the care structures of media, conducted solely by the producers, whereas in my account the live construction is equally shaped by different actors in the three domains (albeit less intentionally). This paradox surfaced most explicitly in chapter 3, where I dealt with the transition from the constellation of liveness in effect for the Original Livestream to that of the New Livestream platform. This example helped me explore how liveness related to processes of institutionalization, which entails that the formlessness of direct real-time content gets molded into a shape condoned by the platform. The "managing" of liveness by producers is necessary because media institutions have come to depend on tightly formatted narratives and program units to generate mass audience interest. In the Original Livestream, it was evident that the "amateurism," which characterized the bulk of its user-generated channels, failed to attract sufficient viewers. These channels, by virtue of being real-time, created immediacy but, due to limited human engagement with them, not liveness. Since the platform was offered to users for free, this created a problem, as the company needed to generate revenue. A new Livestream platform was introduced, which promoted certain production values and targeted more professional content providers. Presumably, then, liveness is a feat achieved by the media industries, built from the interaction between the three domains of liveness. It can be realized only through careful production and management, performed under the influence of sociocultural, technological, and economic forces. The live is not a natural occurrence but is heavily mediated, manifesting itself in a wide range of shapes and forms.

Deliberating on how multiple forms of the live can still constitute a single category, I discussed in the introduction Warren Schmaus, who has argued that categories are bound by their social function. Having explored numerous articulations of the live, I can now establish this function. The "live," I would argue, is the institutionalized product of the interaction between real-time connectivity and sociality, manifesting itself in a series of different configurations of liveness. The manner in which real-time connectivity and sociality interact informs the *value* established through the constellation. It concerns a specification of how an authentic, sociable experience is mediated. This, indeed, is the function that binds these different forms of the live.

At the beginning of this book I mentioned my neighbor Ronny and her visits to the cinema to see simulcasts of performances from London's Royal Opera House. This example readily exposed the complexity of the concept of the live. Exploring the category of the live in greater depth through a series of case studies allowed me to better understand, and expound, the *appeal* of these live-streams, both for the Royal Opera House and the people watching the simulcasts in the cinema. It is not simply that Ronny is offered access to the opera or the ballet, as a technological perspective of the live would have it, but rather that these screenings entitle her, as Scannell would phrase it, to the experience of these performances. In part this is accomplished through the sophisticated camerawork that helps to "presence" her when she attends the simulcast. But salient also is her ability to have the experience of these performances and share her thoughts on them with fellow moviegoers in the cinema hall, on Twitter (should she so wish), and also, later, over the phone with her friend in England. Ronny was made to feel part of an inherently unique and social experience. The Royal Opera House, for its part, capitalizes on this interest in its performances and the sharing of its viewers' experiences.

The cases discussed in the book have also helped me establish that the term "live" can reference different *levels* of mediation. This was already apparent in my brief discussion of the history of the concept "live," which suggested that it could be used to reference live *broadcasting* and live *programming*. In *The Voice*, however, multiple forms of the live were seen to interact to inform a larger construct. Whereas certain episodes of the show were promoted as wholly "live," specific components had in fact been prerecorded. Yet in spite of this, there was no viewer backlash against the live shows for not living up to their promise of liveness—at least, not for this reason. Consequently, these episodes continued to be presented as "live," supporting the idea that they were more inclusive of audience participation than the blind-audition and battle-round episodes.

Considering the existence of multiple reference points for liveness, as I have just discussed, I would argue that, unlike what has been implied in some accounts (Bourdon 2000; Caldwell 2000), liveness does not exist in a "pure" form (or come in a range of different degrees). Its multiplicity clarifies why an understanding of liveness requires situational context and, with it, knowledge of what the "live" is being compared to (since liveness is commonly defined in contrast to a non-live counterpart).

Comparing Broadcast Media to Social Media

My observations on the paradox of liveness have made it possible for the live to serve as a tool for a comparative analysis of broadcast media and social media. They have allowed me to parse out *how* symbolic content was managed on these (media) platforms, in the seemingly common way that characterizes things "live." In chapters 5 and 6, I considered the tensions surrounding the live found in *The Voice* and on Facebook—cases I strategically selected to invite such a comparison. These tensions result from conflicting understandings of the live among contributors from within the three domains of liveness. They allowed me to demystify liveness, grounding it as a sociotechnical construction that media corporations seize upon for added value, capitalizing on a desire for it in the audience. Three different tensions were revealed in the process, linked to a number of related contemporary academic debates. First, there are tensions pertaining to the rhythms and temporalities of broadcast television (in *The Voice*), which I linked here to debates on strategies of series dumping and data-driven decision-making. Second, there are tensions pertaining to audience participation (also in *The Voice*), relating to discussions of producer control over program narratives. And third, there are tensions pertaining to the producer relation to liveness (on Facebook), which I connected to debates on sticky and spreadable media, normative and statistical filtering, and the emerging "Like economy."

The tensions identified in the chapter on *The Voice* concerned the rhythms and temporalities of broadcast television and its control of on-air content. The first tension discussed was that between the schedules of the broadcasters, who tape-delayed the live shows for airing on the West Coast, and the ability of users to discuss programming on social media, which meant that other viewers encountered spoilers online. This tension between the supposed liveness of the broadcast and that of Twitter invited reflection on how, in the broadcast media era, broadcasters used to determine *when* content was to be consumed. But it also allowed me to revisit the constructed nature of liveness. The tension, of course, is specific to countries with multiple time zones, where programs are aired during convenient timeslots (usually, too, the times when advertising costs the most: "primetime")—although popular global sporting events such as the Olympics and the World Cup tend to give rise to such scheduling problems as well. However, it remains to be seen whether video-on-demand and subscription services like Netflix and Amazon Studios will succeed in displacing traditional television's continued push for appointment-TV via strategies such as series dumping and data-driven production development. As Tim Wu, citing novelist John Steinbeck, rightly points out: "It's hard to leave any deeply routined life, even if you hate it" (2013, n.p.). And although television is in fact changing, its transformation is more gradual than people are sometimes made to believe. Moreover, it must not be forgotten that forms of television rely on distinct business models, and that the success of upstarts like Netflix and Amazon Studio relies on viewers' willingness to pay for content (either pay-per-view or on a subscription basis). For many consumers, "free" content supported by advertisers will likely remain preferred.

The second tension found in *The Voice* concerned the gradual decline in opportunities for audience participation in the program over the course of seven seasons. Season 1 offered far more opportunities for audiences to impact onscreen action than was the case in later seasons. The producers, it seems, were reclaiming the program, specifically by limiting the role of social media in the episodes. Their nurturing of audience participation through social media increasingly took a form that allowed only for reactive and active, rather than interactive, forms of user influence. They furthermore carefully controlled how integrations of social media commentary were channeled into the episodes. The need to produce and manage program units discussed here once again highlights the paradox of liveness. There is a need to offer compelling content, that is, for the producers to "work at" the live, and the ability of viewers to affect onscreen action compromised this desire.

In the chapter on Facebook, the tension surrounding the live was centered on a new producer relation to liveness. With users as the focus of the promised liveness, privacy concerns had to be addressed. Indeed, users felt they had little or no control over what and how information was being presented to others. The chapter also tied in with discussions of the changing media environment as media loosened control over content distribution, with users being able to circulate content across their networks. Here the practices of stickiness (organizing attention around a center), familiar from the broadcast media era, were contrasted to those of spreadability (the dispersion of content), which are pervasive in social media. Furthermore, the Facebook case study highlighted the differences between the normative filtering of broadcast media and the statistical filtering done through the platform's algorithms. These sorts of algorithms, widespread in the social media era, determine what content is visible (and with what prominence) for each individual user. Yet, although experiences of Facebook are personalized, people are offered a shared experience of their social networks, and they can discuss the Facebook posts and comments of mutual friends with their friends. Finally, questions were also raised about the emerging "Like economy." With the Like button, Facebook has decentralized data collection: connections are made across the Web, providing data which are then crunched so as to target content to individual users. This individual tracking and targeting of users typify the social media era, and contrast with the business models that dominated the broadcast media.

The social media era is witness to a new concentration of symbolic power in social networks, and to the workings of a new myth, the so-called "myth of us" (Couldry 2014). This myth proposes that these platforms are a natural place for people to come together. However, it is important to critique the assumptions underlying it, for, as Couldry explains, it involves social spaces being rebuilt so as to generate economic value. The tensions surrounding the live I have found in the cases of *The Voice* and Facebook have helped to uncover the *mechanisms of control* through which media manage the production, distribution, and consumption of symbolic content. These mechanisms expose *how* such intermediaries have become "curators of public discourse" (Gillespie 2010). My comparison between *The Voice* and Facebook has shown that in the case of social media, symbolic power is commonly exercised through the management of *distribution* (and to a lesser extent through production). On Facebook, users are primarily responsible for what content is made available, but the platform's algorithms play a critical role in how this content is made visible to others.

The transition to new institutions of the media, I would contend, helps to explain why media studies has witnessed a turn toward the interdisciplinary field of software studies—most notably through the work of Lev Manovich (see Manovich 2013). It also helps to explain the parallel interest in methods of "Big Data" research, such as Richard Rogers's "digital methods" (see Rogers 2013). In our increasingly datafied society, with the computational turn and large collections of data as the byproduct of user interactions with new platforms, algorithms play a crucial role in the distribution of the public's attention. The new media institutions of the social media era actively shape public discourse and, despite their rhetoric, are not a natural occasion of the "social," and reflect only a select group of the general population (people registered for these platforms). As argued by Couldry (2014), the social is in fact being reconstructed via these intermediaries, and the expressive interactions of its users are now commodified. The "myth of us" they perpetuate, I would argue, is founded on a relatively opaque execution of symbolic power. This needs to be unpacked with the help of concepts and theories developed in the aforementioned fields of study.

The Future of Live

Communication and media raise important questions about power, access, and participation (Couldry 2003). In the wake of the "social media revolutions" of the Arab Spring, designated as such by public media celebrating social media (especially Twitter) as tools of empowerment, the exposure of the NSA's mass electronic surveillance program PRISM has revealed that online platforms can equally function as tools of repression. This is just one very obvious example within the current media landscape of how the exercise of power, centered on the collection of data across the Web, affects civil liberties. There are many more such examples, each with different implications for our private and social lives. The approach to liveness that I have proposed invites a critical take on the politics of media, and forewarns readers against accepting their purported neutrality. Tracing how various forces shape participatory spaces creates awareness of the politics involved; such awareness, in turn, offers opportunities for intervention on cultural and legal levels. Analyzing constellations of liveness, indeed, helps to raise important questions and insights into how, and at what cost, people can engage with others and with media institutions.

The book's core argument has been methodological: it has posited the need to treat liveness as a construction. Doing so, I have demonstrated, can help to avoid reductionist assessments of media (e.g., characterizations to the effect that they are ontologically live, live in effect, or ideologically live).

Furthermore, I have shown how deconstructing liveness can offer a rich consideration of how symbolic forms are produced and distributed, disclosing which particular values are bestowed upon specific forms of social interaction or production. As mentioned in the introduction, my perspective on the matter (by virtue of my cases) has been American-centric—as is the canonical literature on the topic. This has had its advantages; for instance, it has allowed me to explore what happens to liveness in situations where viewers are distributed over different time zones. However, it might be useful to explore the role of the live for media in a non-Western context as well. Also delving into questions about the live within the context of public rather than commercial television would be a fruitful line of inquiry. One might wonder, for example, whether public television is served by the live in attempts to highlight its publicness.

Liveness matters to people because it promises them the experience of something (made to seem) relevant—whether a performance on *The Voice*, or the lives of their online social connections. The media industry capitalizes on this desire and works hard to produce and manage such experiences. As media producers continue to assert the superiority of one type of content/medium (labeled "live") over another, and with the desire for experiences still firmly in place, there is good reason to believe that the liveness paradigm in media will persist.

Although it is impossible to predict a future for the category of liveness, it is likely that it is here to stay for at least as long as people desire "authentic" experiences through media, and for as long as media institutions (whether broadcasters or social media platforms) continue to serve as loci of concentrated symbolic power. However, as new models for communicating emerge in the media landscape, new forms of liveness are also likely to surface. Delving into Facebook alone provides a whole range of different live experiments (Live for Facebook Mentions, which allows public figures to share live video with fans, being a more recent example). These future forms will draw on a range of new interactions between real-time connectivity and sociality, and will establish new meanings and values for the live. The live will remain a dynamic category, and will be relied upon to evaluate the quality of communications. It will continue to be associated with a paradox and the tensions that emerge from it. So, rather than bemoan the persistence of the category of the live (see Caldwell 1995; Marriott 2007), scholars should seize on it as a red flag—as a signal to pay attention to the central role that media have claimed for themselves, and how this affects representations of our shared social reality.

Notes

1 The FCC defines broadcast indecency on their website as follows: "language or material that, in context, depicts or describes, in terms patently offensive as measured by contemporary community standards for the broadcast medium, sexual or excretory organs or activities." And profanity is defined as "language so grossly offensive to members of the public who actually hear it as to amount to a nuisance."

2 The Grammy Awards ceremony, whose broadcast was already subjected to a five-second tape delay, began using a more sophisticated tape-delay system, enabling CBS to delete not only inappropriate audio (as was previously the case) but also inappropriate video. The tougher regulation did not, however, extend to news broadcasts.

3 The periodizations "broadcast media era" and "social media era" are not meant to indicate a teleological perspective on media development, as if to suggest that media are becoming increasingly immediate. Nor do I find that it is possible to clearly demarcate these eras in that "periodizations cannot contain history's multiple complexities and contradictions" (Pearson 2011, 107). However, it is useful for considering an important change that has arrived after the bursting of the dot-com bubble: namely, the infiltration of social media platforms into everyday life.

4 This notion is inspired by anthropological approaches to media consumption, such as that of Roger Silverstone, writing about television, that explore media as a cultural process. In Couldry's approach, "ritual" is seen not as the affirmation of what

is shared, in that it maintains or produces social integration, but is connected to the management of conflict and the concealment of social inequality.

5   These questions are inspired by the work of Dirk Eitzen (1995) in which he attempts to define documentary films.

6   Economic power, Thompson (1995) explains, is created through human productive activity where raw materials are extracted and transformed into goods for consumption or sale. Political power concerns the coordination of individuals and the regulation of the patterns of their interaction. Coercive power is about using or threatening physical force to dominate an opponent.

7   See Schäfer (2011) for a short reflection on three different sorts of "critical" accounts of social media: (1) the free labor account, (2) the privacy violation/control and regulation accounts, and (3) the account that positions Web 2.0 platforms as emerging public spheres.

8   O'Reilly's attempt to describe the technological framework for participatory culture through the term Web 2.0 has been criticized. In a podcast interview for IBM in 2006, Tim Berners-Lee, director of the World Wide Web Consortium, was asked if the difference between Web 1.0 and Web 2.0 was one of connecting computers against connecting people. His response was that the Web was meant to be a collaborative space for social interaction all along (in Farber 2006, n.p.), and Web 2.0 built on the existing standards of the Web, simply adding some Java Script (see also Scholz 2008; Berry 2011). The term itself is problematic because of its teleological connotations, suggesting that the Web is constantly being improved, moving toward ever-greater sociality (van den Boomen 2007). Whereas I agree with Berners-Lee's criticism, specifically where it concerns Web 2.0 having brought only limited technological innovation, I do find, as van Dijck does, that there has been an evident shift in online services. Between 1.0 and 2.0, there has been a development from networked communication, functioning as channels, to networked sociality, mediating relations (2013a). By the same token, the ways that people can interact and participate with one another have changed.

9   In addressing Jenkins's work specifically, Matt Hills has pointed out that in discussing reading and talking about texts as a form of production, he has hollowed out the concept—as in this account, the only way not to be producing is by not consuming media at all (Hills 2002, 36). Besides this, there are three more problems with Jenkins's work. First, on the macro level, he offers a fairly romantic account of participatory culture and,

in doing so, downplays the top-down forces that shape user activity (Burgess and Green 2009; Müller 2009; Schäfer 2011). The second problem concerns the fact that for Jenkins, convergence is about the struggles between top-down corporate activities and bottom-up user practices (Jenkins 2006, 18). As Müller correctly points out, he thus sketches a "moral opposition" between the empowerment of user practices versus the oppressiveness of corporate enterprise (2009, 59)—one that very much echoes the opposition between the utopian and dystopian tendencies characterized above. Third, Jenkins's focus on fan activities fails to account for user-production that does not take place in relation to existing media production (Schäfer 2011).

10 Connected hereto is how practices like data mining and user profiling have brought to the fore issues of privacy (Fuchs 2012; Zimmer 2008). Part of the problem has been that users do not know what data is being collected and/or have limited control as to how this data is being used (e.g., for targeted advertising).

11 With these particular concepts, beyond those used by Schäfer, I am able to make explicit the fact that these domains reciprocally affect each other—particularly in that an interest in spaces of participation, rather than simply technology, helps to posit the platforms I study as products of various forces.

12 Rather than, as Durkheim has suggested, through the social causes of their individual and collective representations.

13 In his book, Gray differentiates between official and fan-created paratexts. The focus of my research is on the meanings offered by the platforms themselves.

14 I have deliberately replaced the term "constraints," as used by Müller, with "forces," as I want to draw attention to both constraints and affordances in my analyses.

15 My method here is similar to that which van Dijck (2013a) proposes for the platform analysis. She specifically argues for complementing a political economy approach (focused on platform ownership, governance, and business models) with procedures from ANT (focused on platform technology, users/usage, and content). However, I prefer the concept of space of participation, as it allows me to explore how various forces come to shape frameworks of action.

16 I, however, agree with Bucher that it "is not necessarily [important] to know every technical detail of how a system works, but to be able to understand some of the logics or principles of their functioning in order to critically engage with the ways in which systems work on a theoretical level" (2012, 14).

17   "Mogulus—How It Works," YouTube, posted May 10, 2007, http://www.youtube.com/watch?v=4gVjPHAUpBo.

18   In Mogulus's explanation of "live broadcast," live cameras were contrasted with video clips. This distinction shows that the Mogulus platform's constellation of liveness was informed by another "live" construct as well: that of the live camera. For now, I leave this insight aside, but I pick it up again in chapter 5, where I trace how multiple constructions of the live can be embedded in a larger constellation.

19   It is worth emphasizing here that I am not out to reiterate a reductive producer-consumer binary (let my use of the concept of 'space of participation' be a testament to this). However, for the sake of clarity, I have used these terms/positions to delineate which practices were afforded by the platforms.

20   When the platform was still named Mogulus, it was only 500 kbps, because streaming at higher bandwidths was not yet an option.

21   A snapshot of the website from June 15, 2009, shows Procaster being announced as a new feature. Webcaster is mentioned in the forum for the first time in September 2009.

22   This specifically concerns the 20.2.28 version of the software.

23   There is some conflict in the numbers concerning online video between Nielsen and comScore. For my purposes, these discrepancies are not troubling, as my point is that Haot uses such figures (in this case, from comScore) to promote his own enterprise.

24   The reason for this is that from this moment on, the guide featured channels only if they had sought verification. In light of what I have written here on the space of participation, I suspect that only operators of channels exceeding fifty concurrent viewers would have taken the effort of seeking this verification. Although this is an inference on my part, it is confirmed (among other confirmations) by how the company's CEO, in what follows, reflects on platform use. Something to take into account also is that a channel's very listing could have played a role in its attracting viewers, or keeping viewing rates up.

25   Again I must note here that exploring user responses is not about conducting representative research, but about locating comments and/or practices that reveal something about the liveness of the platform.

26   "Live or pre-recorded," comment posted on October 24, 2010, http://www.livestream.com/forum/showthread.php?t=5271.

27   "How can you tell if it is really live?," comment posted on November 16, 2011, http://www.livestream.com/forum/showthread.php?t=8355.

28 This observation does not, of course, reveal anything about the proportion of user-generated channels, as many of those may simply not have been listed.

29 In an earlier interview (TechCrunch 2011), Haot made a similar observation: "Bloggers really don't have the resources, monetization, the content, the audience, so they would try [to set up a channel] and it would stop. But then, every time an event used the platform, you know, it was very successful. It made sense and it would keep happening every time at all of them."

30 He even suggested that although viewers may prefer to be present at the actual event, the experience of Livestream offers a good alternative.

31 In addition to the platform itself, I make use here of the Livestream website (which at the time centered on the race), as well as the promotional video for the race and a PDF document on the website entitled "What is the New Livestream?" that explored the platform and its values.

32 This may have been the reason why a "producer account," at this time, went for $45 a month (price as noted on June 17, 2012; source: "Livestream Platforms Plans & Pricing," Livestream, n.d., http://new.livestream.com/broadcast-live/pricing-plans).

33 This account went for $269 a month for the channel plan (best for individuals), $962 a month for the network plan (best for organizations); for the custom plan (best for large events) a price arrangement had to be made.

34 "Audio Interfaces," eJamming, n.d., http://ejamming.com/audio-interfaces/.

35 It should be noted that in contrast to what is claimed in early statements about the internet being an "electronic frontier," geography still matters: the efficacy of internet communications depends on the location in real space of data and data consumers, and on the geographical distribution of the underlying internet hardware through which the data travels (Goldsmith and Wu 2008, 55).

36 By comparison, avoiding gaps in conversation over the telephone, for instance, requires a round-trip delay of 100 msec at the most.

37 See "NINJAM," Cockos Incorporated, n.d., http://www.cockos.com/ninjam/.

38 This was observed by William, in a January 17, 2010, comment on "Fender and eJamming Audio Unveil Synchronized, Streaming Jamming Software," Premierguitar, posted on January 15, 2010, http://www.premierguitar.com/Magazine/Issue/Daily/News/Fender_and_eJamming_Audio_Unveil_Synchronized_Streaming_Jamming_Software.

39   See "NINJAM."
40   Driessen et al. (2011) have found that these methods tend to backfire. As the processing time for synchronization, compression, and decompression are increased, so is latency, and they therefore find that peer-to-peer connection is not always beneficial to users.
41   Whereas such practice suggests that there is some sense of community, the reality cannot be ignored that only two users replied to the question that was raised.
42   Participants could determine otherwise but had to do so in writing prior to the session.
43   Although exact numbers are of lesser interest to me here, it might be worth pointing out that the eJamming forum was divided into four sections: "Help," "News," "Discussion," and "Community." Among those, the "Help" tab was by far the most popular in terms of user activity, meaning that it had the most threads and attracted the most views. The most popular permanent title within this section, in terms of views, was "Port Issues." In terms of the amount of threads and posts, it was "Feature Requests." The "Help" section led in terms of user-initiated activity, counting a total number of 85 threads, 137 posts, and 4,809 views. To put this into perspective, under "Community" there were only 7 threads, 8 posts, and 140 views. (I should add here that I am well aware that the view count on the forum concerned total views rather than unique ones, so the numbers may have been generated by a small group of active users. Also, in 2011, co-founder Alan Glueckman was not only often available for chatting in the Lobby, he also actively initiated threads and frequently replied to posts. For those reasons, the data are not used here as a starting point for far-reaching conclusions, but merely to provide a general impression as to what topics were popular among eJamming users.)
44   February 14, 2011, comment on Gadi R, "Online Jam Sessions vs Ejamming Opinions?," posted February 13, 2011, http://forums.musicplayer.com/ubbthreads.php/topics/2273653/Re_Online_Jam_Sessions_vs_Ejam.
45   March 5, 2011, comment on Gadi R, "Online Jam Sessions vs Ejamming Opinions?"
46   March 11, 2011, comment on "Fender and eJamming Audio Unveil Synchronized, Streaming Jamming Software," Premierguitar, posted on January 15, 2010, http://www.premierguitar.com/Magazine/Issue/Daily/News/Fender_and_eJamming_Audio_Unveil_Synchronized_Streaming_Jamming_Software.
47   March 5, 2011, comment on Gadi R, "Online Jam Sessions vs Ejamming Opinions?"

48   I signed up for a one-month trial on April 4, 2011, and fol-
     lowed this up with a membership for three months thereafter.
     During this time, I noticed that Glueckman was frequently
     online as ThunderPup44. Of course, working from The Neth-
     erlands rather than the United States, my time zone may well
     have played a role in the lack of users online when I logged
     on. Nonetheless, online comments show I was certainly not the
     only user who experienced it this way.

49   Posted in January 2011.

50   The format of the program was purchased by the NBC network
     from the Dutch company Talpa Productions; the program was
     first aired in the United States on April 26, 2011.

51   This section of the chapter was the basis of my article "THE
     VOICE: Über das 'Soziale' des sozialen Fernsehens," co-written
     with Eggo Müller. It was published in German in 2012 (van
     Es and Müller 2012).

52   To Uricchio, this first period, which he calls the "broadcast
     era," constitutes television's stable period and continues to
     frame common conceptions of what television is (Uricchio
     2009, 27). These conceptions are aptly captured by the meta-
     phors attributed to television in TV theory; television, flow and
     broadcasting (Gripsrud 1998).

53   It should be pointed out that these figures may be tainted
     because they take into account only traditional channels of
     consumption (although Nielsen now does include time-delayed
     replays in its figures). The figures on *The Big Bang Theory* are
     taken from the Nielsen website; see http://www.nielsen.com/us/
     en/insights/news/2015/tops-of-2015-tv-and-social-media.html.

54   Al Jazeera English, for instance, has opted for an aggressive
     use of social media in its news reporting. In May 2011, it
     launched the daily television program *The Stream*, which con-
     structs news by harnessing user-generated content and tapping
     into online discussions on social media platforms, using the
     content curation platform Storify.

55   On Twitter's corporate blog, the successes of its marriage to
     television are heavily celebrated and promoted.

56   Both have since been suspended.

57   When contestants were eliminated, their activity seemingly
     ceased on blogs hosted on the NBC website, but all remained
     active on Facebook and Twitter.

58   Producers are not always successful in their attempts to
     implement certain hashtags. This was evident with *The
     World According to Paris*, where the onscreen tag #TheWorld-
     AccordingtoParis, appearing throughout the show in the
     upper-right hand corner of the screen, was less popular than

the user-driven tag #Paris which emerged naturally (Bergman 2011b).

59 More precisely, it was broadcast first in the Eastern and Central time zones and then three hours later on Pacific Standard (or Daylight) Time, but here I use "East Coast" and "West Coast" as shorthand for these broadcast times, though not all areas in these time zones are on the coasts.

60 For a comprehensive understanding of the Twitter platform and its space of participation, see Van Dijck (2011).

61 This is true unless privacy settings have been set to restrict access.

62 This conclusion is based on comments I found on Twitter, in which users would ask how they could get their tweet on air (in the V-Room).

63 With regard to research ethics, I did not seek informed consent from those tweeting about the show. After careful deliberation, I believed the academic benefit of being able to cite my sources outweighed the need for their anonymity. First, unlike many other platforms with complicated privacy settings, Twitter offers a clear option to users between having their tweets be public or protected. The tweets I collected are only from users who have their tweets set to public. Second, I only cite tweets that make explicit use of the official hashtag of *The Voice*. I see this as an explicit choice by the user to make it part of a public discussion. Lastly, my research topic is not controversial or sensitive in nature.

64 This usually happened via phrasings such as "We are live," or "Welcome back to *The Voice* live."

65 The speech concerned the withdrawal of troops from Afghanistan.

66 It here concerns the episode broadcast on June 7, 2011.

67 This of course is almost surely not the case: people who tweet about a show tend to send out a lot of tweets.

68 My search focused on the period between May 18 and June 16, 2011.

69 I single out this episode for no particular reason; all of the live shows demonstrated this same pattern in Twitter use.

70 This corresponds to how the Twitter company itself characterizes real-time conversations (http://media.twitter.com/twitter-tv).

71 This is true for all the tweets I collected, not just those containing "thevoice" and "live."

72 Twittercounter provided this data. The reason why Christina Aguilera has been excluded here is that she did not have a Twitter account prior to the show.

73   The dates assessed here are April 24, 2011, and June 29, 2011.
74   The increase in followers, of course, cannot be traced to their exposure on *The Voice* alone, but the visible boosts following airings points to a certain correlation.
75   The conclusion was that the iTunes songs were not "live recordings"—yet another live construct that could be explored in more depth.
76   Much to the surprise of the public, it released the *Breaking Bad* prequel *Better Call Saul* in 2015 at the pace of one episode a week, at least in Europe and Latin America. The deal with Sony Pictures Television stipulated that U.S. subscribers would receive the episodes after the show finished its run on AMC.
77   I explore these changes and the friction that arises from them in a separate article (see van Es 2015).
78   I here implicitly reference the three "degrees" of user influence on media production proposed by Gunn Sara Enli (2012): reactive, active, and interactive. Respectively, these refer to low influence on the production process (as in quizzes and polls), accumulative influence on production (as in voting), and high influence on parts of the production.
79   I would say this relation is not so much new as it is a type of relation that has become more dominant in the social media era.
80   Aside from the different manifestations of the platform, there are multiple routes by which to "access" it. In this chapter I look at Facebook set to the primary language of English (US) and visited via a Mozilla Firefox browser, unless otherwise noted.
81   This is the situation as it presented itself in November 2012, with me using a Firefox browser to navigate the site.
82   When something happens that affects the user in question, a light blue square pops up next to the text with a dark blue number featured in the square, signaling (an) unattended item(s).
83   Like Bucher (2012) I find that to engage with it on a theoretical level it is more important to understand the logics of how they function rather than to know every technical detail.
84   The penetration was 42.3 percent in Australia and Oceania and 34.33 percent in South America. Facebook has a comparatively low population penetration in Asia (6.89 percent) and Africa (5.35 percent); in the former, other social networking websites have taken the lead.
85   Timeline replaced the Wall feature as of December 2011.
86   In popular media, Twitter was said to have broken the news first. Reflecting on this incident, Salmon (2011) writes critically

of the *New York Times* in that their ombudsman claimed to have broken the news on their website, and was unwilling to credit how the news had broken on Twitter. Salmon furthermore provided an interesting visualization of how the news spread on Twitter, identifying the most interesting and influential actors on the platform.

87   In personal correspondence, Jim Gibbons rightfully pointed out how—in an age of media convergence—such a poll drastically oversimplifies matters. Although he had gotten the news from the televised address (which would have been his response to the poll), thanks to Twitter speculations he knew what was going to be announced beforehand.

88   In chapter 3, the Original Livestream also exemplified this "new" relation to the live. I discuss the social-media-era phenomenon of algorithmic intervention in more depth just below.

89   They identify the following central trackers (named in no particular order): Google Analytics, Google Adsense, Google+1, DoubleClick, Twitter Button, Facebook Connect, Facebook Social Plugins, Quantcast, Scorecard Research Beacon, and Omniture.

Resources

Online Videos

Beet.TV. 2011. "Max Haot on Livestream's High Average Video Viewing Time." *Dailymotion*. Posted April 1. http:// www.dailymotion.com/video/xgee4w_max-haot-on-livestream-s -high-average-video-viewing-time_tech.

dizzytree13. 2009. "ONLINESESSIONSSUCK." *YouTube*. Posted June 17. http://www.youtube.com/watch?v=yXbartfWwvU&NR =1.

TechCrunch. 2011. "Livestream's Haot: 'You Have to Be Able to Say I Was Wrong & Do It in a Very Public Way.'" *TechCrunch*. November 12. http://techcrunch.com/2011/11/12/founder-stories -livestreams-haot-you-have-to-be-able-to-say-i-was-wrong-do-it -in-a-very-public-way/.

Tilzy.TV. 2007. "Mogulus." *YouTube*. Posted November 21. https:// www.youtube.com/watch?v=0FtHpOPdQv0.

Platforms, Forums, and Weblogs

eJamming: http://www.ejamming.com

eJamming Facebook page: https://www.facebook.com/#!/pages/ eJamming/368668856036

eJamming RADiiO project: http://www.cartmania.org.uk/ejamming/ about/

Facebook: https://www.facebook.com
Justin.tv: http://www.justin.tv
Musicplayer: http://forums.musicplayer.com/
The New Livestream: http://new.livestream.com
Ninbot: http://ninbot.com
The Original Livestream: http://www.livestream.com
Premierguitar: http://www.premierguitar.com
Stickam: http://www.stickam.com
YouTube: http://www.youtube.com

Television

The Voice (seasons 1 to 7). 2011–2014. Executive producers John de Mol, Mark Burnett, Audrey Morrissey, Stijn Bakkers, and Lee Metzger. NBC.

Tweets

Bailey, Tiffany (@lilmstiffy). "Weather service I need you to stop interrupting #TheVoice to talk about this tornado watch. I get it, but my show is on live, let me live!" June 21, 2011, 21:49.

Diana (@dyeisag). "WTH MAN! These lives [*sic*] shows aren't really live! People need to keep their mouths shut until each time zone watches the show #TheVoice." June 29, 2011, 21:08.

Egaas, Aaron (@aegaas). "Hey live TV shows, don't tell your west coasters to go on Twitter only to have your show spoiled. #fail #theVoice #fail." June 29, 2011, 22:29.

Holder, Mitchell (@mitchellholder). "Adam Levine is a talentless live singing sham. Pales in comparison to the other coaches. #TheVoice." June 28, 2011, 21:05.

(@Inspired_Panda) "@bitchcraftradio because it isn't live on the west coast (aired earlier on the east coast) #thevoice." June 29, 2011, 22:47.

Knight, Erin (@Indigoperry). "#TheVoice has made watching TV live relevant again! #SorryDVR This show is so much fun!" June 14, 2011, 21:02.

Senna, Matthew (@msenna). "#thevoice ruined the results by not having a live finale. With social media you can't keep results secret for 3hrs!" June 29, 2011, 23:35.

Varner, Jared (@jaredmv70). "First time watching #thevoice live. Now I remember why. I hate commercials!" June 21, 2011, 21:09.

Welch, Alice (@TheWriterBabe). "RT @ SwiftyGuy13: Blake sounds as good live as he does in studio. Not many artists can do that! #TheVoice." June 21, 2011, 22:35.

Zielinski, Becca (@BeccaZeels). "Hey Carlson Daly, is #thevoice live?...how many times are you gonna remind us? Probably gotta remind @blakeshelton so he watches his mouth." June 14, 2011, 22:00.

References

Alang, Navneet. 2010. "We're Not Fooled: Ignoring Privacy Is Facebook's Business Model." *Techi.com*. May 28. http://www.techi.com/2010/05/were-not-fooled-ignoring-privacy-is-facebooks-business-model/.

Anderson, Benedict. 2006. *Imagined Communities: Reflections on the Origin and Spread of Nationalism*. Rev. ed. New York: Verso.

Andrejevic, Mark. 2008. "Watching Television without Pity: The Productivity of Online Fans." *Television & New Media* 9 (1): 24–46.

———. 2009. "Exploiting YouTube: Contradictions of User-Generated Labor." In *The YouTube Reader*, edited by Pelle Snickars and Patrick Vonderau, 406–23. Mediehistoriskt Arkiv 12. Stockholm: National Library of Sweden.

Auslander, Philip. 2008. *Liveness: Performance in a Mediatized Culture*. 2nd ed. New York: Routledge.

———. 2012. "Digital Liveness: A Historico-Philosophical Perspective." *PAJ: A Journal of Performance and Art* 34 (3): 3–11. doi:10.1162/PAJJ_a_00106.

Baldwin, Roberto. 2012. "Netflix's Big Data Gamble to Become the HBO of Streaming | Gadget Lab | Wired.com." *Wired*. November 29. http://www.wired.com/2012/11/netflix-data-gamble/.

Baumgartner, Jody C., and Jonathan S. Morris. 2010. "MyFace-Tube Politics: Social Networking Web Sites and Political Engagement of Young Adults." *Social Science Computer Review* 28 (1): 24–44. doi:10.1177/0894439309334325.

Baym, Nancy K. 2000. *Tune In, Log On: Soaps, Fandom, and Online Community*. New Media Cultures. Thousand Oaks, CA: Sage Publications.

Bennett, James. 2011. "Introduction: Television as Digital Media." In *Television as Digital Media*, edited by James Bennett and Niki Strange, 1–30. Console-Ing Passions. Durham, NC: Duke University Press.

Bergman, Cory. 2011a. "Even 'Doctor Who' Can't Time-Shift Social Media." *LostRemote*. www.adweek.com/lostremote/even-doctor -who-cant-time-shift-social-media/18643.

———. 2011b. "Paris Hilton Flaunts Social Media for TV Show Premiere." *LostRemote*. June 2. http://www.adweek.com/ lostremote/paris-hilton-flaunts-social-media-for-show-premiere/ 20181.

Berry, David M. 2011. *The Philosophy of Software: Code and Mediation in the Digital Age*. New York: Palgrave Macmillan.

Beyer, Yngvil, Gunn Sara Enli, Arnt Johan Maaso, and Espen Ytreberg. 2007. "Small Talk Makes a Big Difference: Recent Developments in Interactive, SMS-Based Television." *Television & New Media* 8 (3): 213–34. doi:10.1177/1527476407301642.

Boddy, William. 2003. "Redefining the Home Screen: Technological Convergence as Trauma and Business Plan." In *Rethinking Media Change: The Aesthetics of Television*, edited by David Thorburn and Henry Jenkins, 191–200. Cambridge, MA: MIT Press.

Bolter, Jay David, and Richard A. Grusin. 2000. *Remediation: Understanding New Media*. Cambridge, MA: MIT Press.

Bourdon, Jérôme. 2000. "Live Television is Still Alive: On Television as an Unfulfilled Promise." *Media, Culture & Society* 22 (5): 531–56. doi:10.1177/016344300022005001.

boyd, danah. 2008. "Facebook's Privacy Trainwreck: Exposure, Invasion, and Social Convergence." *Convergence* 14 (14): 13–20.

boyd, danah, and Eszter Hargittai. 2010. "Facebook Privacy Settings: Who Cares?" *First Monday* 15 (8). http://firstmonday.org/ article/view/3086/2589.

Bruns, Axel, and Stefan Stieglitz. 2012. "Quantitative Approaches to Comparing Communication Patterns on Twitter." *Journal of Technology in Human Services* 30 (3–4): 160–85.

Bucher, Taina. 2012. "Want to Be on the Top? Algorithmic Power and the Threat of Invisibility on Facebook." *New Media & Society* 14 (7): 1164–80. doi:10.1177/1461444812440159.

———. 2015. "Networking, or What the Social Means in Social Media." *Social Media + Society* 1 (1). doi:10.1177/ 2056305115578138.

Burgess, Jean, and Joshua Green. 2009. *YouTube: Online Video and Participatory Culture*. Digital Media and Society Series. Malden, MA: Polity.

Caldwell, John Thornton. 1995. *Televisuality: Style, Crisis, and Authority in American Television*. Communication, Media, and Culture. New Brunswick, NJ: Rutgers University Press.

———. 2000. "Live Slippages: Performing and Programming Televisual Liveness." In *Live Is Life*, edited by Gerd Hallenberger and Helmut Schanze, 21–46. Baden-Baden: Nomos.

Carlson, Nicholas. 2008. "YouTube Plans To Launch Live-Streaming November 22." *Business Insider.* November 6. http://www.businessinsider.com/2008/11/youtube-plans-to-launch-live-streaming-november-22.

Castells, Manuel. 2009. *Communication Power*. New York: Oxford University Press.

Cianci, Bob. 2015. "eJamming." *Guitarcoach Magazine*. June 11. https://guitarcoachmag.com/magazine-issue-02/ejamming/.

Constine, Josh. 2013. "Facebook Redesign Kills Ticker, Almost." *TechCrunch*. March 8. http://techcrunch.com/2013/03/08/facebook-ticker-disappeared/.

Couldry, Nick. 2000. *The Place of Media Power: Pilgrims and Witnesses of the Media Age*. Comedia. New York: Routledge.

———. 2003. *Media Rituals: A Critical Approach*. London: Routledge.

———. 2004. "Liveness, 'Reality,' and the Mediated Habitus from Television to the Mobile Phone." *Communication Review* 7 (4): 353–61. doi:10.1080/10714420490886952.

———. 2012. *Media, Society, World: Social Theory and Digital Media Practice*. Malden, MA: Polity.

———. 2014. "The Myth of 'Us': Digital Networks, Political Change and the Production of Collectivity." *Information, Communication & Society* 18 (6): 608–26.

Davidson, Drew. 2010. *Cross-Media Communications: An Introduction to the Art of Creating Integrated Media Experiences*. 10th ed. Pittsburgh: ETC Press.

Davis, Kevin. 2008. "Latency and Jitter—Highlight." *Highlight: CA Technologies Blog*. June 23. http://54.85.17.110/2008/06/23/latency-and-jitter/.

Dayan, Daniel, and Elihu Katz. 1992. *Media Events: The Live Broadcasting of History*. Cambridge, MA: Harvard University Press.

Deller, Ruth. 2011. "Twitter On: Audience Research and Participation Using Twitter." *Participations: Journal of Audience & Reception Studies* 8 (1): 216–45.

Dixon, Steve. 2007. *Digital Performance: A History of New Media in Theater, Dance, Performance Art, and Installation*. Cambridge, MA: MIT Press.

Drell, Lauren. 2011. "The Voice: How a TV Show Became a 24/7 Social Media Conversation." *Mashable.* June 15. http://mashable. com/2011/06/15/the-voice-social-media-nbc/.

Driessen, Peter F., Thomas E. Darcie, and Bipin Pillay. 2011. "The Effects of Network Delay on Tempo in Musical Performance." *Computer Music Journal* 35 (1): 76–89. doi:10.1162/COMJ_a _00041.

Dumenco, Simon. 2011. "7 Things You Need to Know About 'Social TV' Right Now." *AdAge.* September 19. http://adage.com/ article/the-media-guy/social-tv/229845/.

Dybwad, Barb. 2009. "Facebook's Live Feed Redesign Goes Live Today." *Mashable.* October 23. http://mashable.com/2009/10/23/ facebook-redesign-2/.

Edelsburg, Natan. 2011. "The Team That Made 'The Voice' a Social TV Hit." *LostRemote.* July 7. http://www.adweek. com/lostremote/the-social-team-that-made-the-voice-possible/ 21085.

Eitzen, Dirk. 1995. "When Is a Documentary?: Documentary as a Mode of Reception." *Cinema Journal* 35 (1): 81–102.

Ellis, John. 2000. *Seeing Things: Television in the Age of Uncertainty.* New York: I. B. Tauris.

Enli, Gunn Sara. 2012. "From Parasocial Interaction to Social TV: Analysing the Host–Audience Relationship in Multi-Platform Productions." *Northern Lights: Film & Media Studies Yearbook* 10: 123–37.

Erickson, Christine. 2012. "Facebook Statistics by Continent." *Social Bakers.* October 8. http://www.socialbakers.com/countries/ continents.

———. 2013. "Is Netflix Hurting Television Buzz?" *Mashable.* March 25. http://mashable.com/2013/03/25/netflix-television -buzz-infographic/.

Farber, Dan. 2006. "Web 2.0 = a Piece of Jargon." *ZDNet.* August 31. http://www.zdnet.com/article/web-2-0-a-piece-of-jargon/.

Fenton, Natalie. 2012. "The Internet and Social Networking." In *Misunderstanding the Internet,* edited by James Curran, Natalie Fenton, and Des Freedman, 121–48. Communication and Society. New York: Routledge.

Feuer, Jane. 1983. "The Concept of Live Television: Ontology as Ideology." In *Regarding Television: Critical Approaches—An Anthology,* edited by Ann Kaplan, 12–21. Los Angeles: American Film Institute.

Fletcher, Dan. 2010. "We're Not Fooled: Ignoring Privacy Is Facebook's Business Model." *Time.* May 20. http://content.time.com/ time/magazine/article/0,9171,1990798,00.html.

Friedman, James. 2002. "Introduction." In *Reality Squared: Televisual Discourse on the Real*, edited by James Friedman, 1–24. New Brunswick, NJ: Rutgers University Press.

Fuchs, Christian. 2011. "Web 2.0, Prosumption, and Surveillance." *Surveillance and Society* 8 (3): 288–309.

———. 2012. "The Political Economy of Privacy on Facebook." *Television & New Media* 13 (2): 139–59. doi:10.1177/1527476411415699.

Galloway, Alexander R. 2006. *Protocol: How Control Exists after Decentralization*. Cambridge, MA: MIT Press.

Gehl, Robert W. 2013. "'Why I Left Facebook': Stubbornly Refusing to Not Exist Even after Opting Out of Mark Zuckerberg's Social Graph." In *Unlike Us Reader: Social Media Monopolies and Their Alternatives*, edited by Geert Lovink and Miriam Rasch, 220–38. Amsterdam: Institute of Network Cultures.

Genette, Gérard. 1991. "Introduction to the Paratext." *New Literary History* 22 (2): 261–72.

Gerlitz, Carolin, and Anne Helmond. 2013. "The Like Economy: Social Buttons and the Data-Intensive Web." *New Media & Society* 15 (8): 1348–65. doi:10.1177/1461444812472322.

Gibson, James J. 1977. "The Theory of Affordances." In *Perceiving, Acting, and Knowing*, edited by Robert Shaw and John Bransford. Hoboken, NJ: John Wiley.

Gillan, Jennifer. 2011. *Television and New Media: Must-Click TV*. New York: Routledge.

Gillespie, Tarleton. 2010. "The Politics of 'Platforms'." *New Media & Society* 12 (3): 347–64. doi:10.1177/1461444809342738.

———. 2015. "Platforms Intervene." *Social Media + Society* 1 (1). doi:10.1177/2056305115580479.

Glass, Suzanne. 2007. "Company Profile: eJamming." *Indie-Music.com*. June 5. http://www.indie-music.com/modules.php?name=News&file=print&sid=5998.

Goldsmith, Jack L., and Tim Wu. 2008. *Who Controls the Internet?: Illusions of a Borderless World*. New York: Oxford University Press.

Gordhamer, Soren. 2011. "Will the New Facebook Lead to Information Overload?" *Mashable*. October 27. http://mashable.com/2011/10/07/facebook-information-overload/.

Gorman, Bill. 2011. "2010–2011 Season Broadcast Primetime Show Viewership Averages." *TVbytheNumbers*. June 1. http://tvbythenumbers.zap2it.com/2011/06/01/2010-11-season-broadcast-primetime-show-viewership-averages/94407/.

Gray, Jonathan. 2010. *Show Sold Separately: Promos, Spoilers, and Other Media Paratexts*. New York: New York University Press.

Gray, Jonathan, and Amanda D. Lotz. 2012. *Television Studies.* Cambridge, MA: Polity.

Greene, Kate. 2007. "Jam Online in Real Time." *MIT Technology Review.* May 25. http://www.technologyreview.com/news/407965/jam-online-in-real-time/.

Grint, Keith, and Steve Woolgar. 1997. *The Machine at Work: Technology, Work, and Organization.* Cambridge: Blackwell; Malden, MA: Polity.

Gripsrud, Jostein. 1998. "Television, Broadcasting, Flow: Key Metaphors in TV Theory." In *The Television Studies Book*, edited by Christine Geraghty and David Lusted, 17–23. London: Arnold.

———. 2010. "Television in the Digital Public Sphere." In *Relocating Television: Television in the Digital Context*, by Jostein Gripsrud, 3–26. New York: Routledge.

Grossman, Lev. 2010. "Person of the Year 2010: Mark Zuckerberg." *Time.* December 15. http://content.time.com/time/specials/packages/article/0,28804,2036683_2037183_2037185,00.html.

Guthrie, Marisa. 2011. "Oscar Ratings Fall From Last Year." *Hollywood Reporter.* February 28. http://www.hollywoodreporter.com/news/oscar-ratings-fall-last-year-162408.

Hallinan, Blake, and Ted Striphas. 2014. "Recommended for You: The Netflix Prize and the Production of Algorithmic Culture." *New Media & Society*, June. doi:10.1177/1461444814538646.

Halperin, Shirley. 2011. "How Twitter Raises 'The Voice's Ratings." *Billboard.* June 21. http://www.billboard.com/biz/articles/news/tv-film/1177396/how-twitter-raises-the-voices-ratings.

Hampton, Keith N., Lauren Sessions Goulet, Lee Rainie, and Kristen Purcell. 2011. "Social Networking Sites and Our Lives." Washington, DC: Pew Research Center. http://www.pewinternet.org/files/old-media//Files/Reports/2011/PIP%20-%20Social%20networking%20sites%20and%20our%20lives.pdf.

Harries, Dan, ed. 2004. *The New Media Book.* Reprint. London: British Film Institute.

Hern, Alex. 2015. "Facebook Relaxes 'Real Name' Policy in Face of Protest." *Guardian.* November 2. http://www.theguardian.com/technology/2015/nov/02/facebook-real-name-policy-protest.

Heath, Stephen, and Gillian Skirrow. 1977. "Television: A World in Action." *Screen* 18 (2): 7–59.

Hicks, Matt. 2010. "Building the Social Web Together." Facebook. *Notes by Facebook.* April 21. https://www.facebook.com/notes/facebook/building-the-social-web-together/383404517130.

Highfield, Tim, Stephen Harrington, and Axel Bruns. 2013. "Twitter as a Technology for Audiencing and Fandom: The #Eurovision Phenomenon." *Information, Communication & Society* 16 (3): 315–39. doi:10.1080/1369118X.2012.756053.

Hill, Kashmir. 2012. "Now That Facebook Is Charging Users, Why Not Offer These Paid Features?" *Forbes*. October 8. http://www.forbes.com/sites/kashmirhill/2012/10/08/now-that-facebook-is-charging-users-why-not-offer-these-paid-features/.

Hills, Matt. 2002. *Fan Cultures*. New York: Routledge.

Hopkins, Mark. 2008. "Mogulus Officially Goes Freemium." *Mashable*. December 8. http://mashable.com/2008/12/04/mogulus-pro-services/.

Horton, Donald, and Richard Wohl. 1956. "Mass Communication and Para-Social Interaction. Observations on Intimacy at a Distance." *Psychiatry: Interpersonal and Biological Processes* 19 (3): 215–29.

Hutchby, Ian. 2001. "Technologies, Texts and Affordances." *Sociology* 35 (2): 441–56. doi:10.1177/S0038038501000219.

Jacobs, Jason. 2000. *The Intimate Screen: Early British Television Drama*. Oxford: Oxford University Press; New York: Clarendon.

Jenkins, Henry. 2003. "Transmedia Storytelling." *MIT Technology Review*. January 15. http://www.technologyreview.com/news/401760/transmedia-storytelling/.

———. 2006. *Convergence Culture: Where Old and New Media Collide*. New York: New York University Press.

———. 2013. "Kickstarting Veronica Mars: A Conversation on the Future of Television (Part Two)." *Confessions of an Aca-Fan*. March 27. http://henryjenkins.org/2013/03/kickstarting-veronica-mars-a-conversation-on-the-future-of-television-part-two.html.

———. 2014. "Rethinking 'Rethinking Convergence/Culture.'" *Cultural Studies* 28 (2): 267–97. doi:10.1080/09502386.2013.801579.

Jenkins, Henry, Sam Ford, and Joshua Green. 2013. *Spreadable Media: Creating Value and Meaning in a Networked Culture*. New York: New York University Press.

Jonietz, Erika. 2010. "Making TV Social, Virtually." *MIT Technology Review*. November 1. http://www.technologyreview.com/news/417055/making-tv-social-virtually/.

Kaplan, Andreas M., and Michael Haenlein. 2010. "Users of the World, Unite! The Challenges and Opportunities of Social Media." *Business Horizons* 53 (1): 59–68. doi:10.1016/j.bushor.2009.09.003.

Keating, Gina. 2013. *Netflixed: The Epic Battle for America's Eyeballs*. New York: Penguin.

Kennedy, Jenny. 2013. "Rhetorics of Sharing: Data, Imagination, and Desire." In *Unlike Us Reader: Social Media Monopolies and Their Alternatives*, edited by Geert Lovink and Miriam Rasch, 127–45. Amsterdam: Institute of Network Cultures.

Kim, Jin. 2012. "The Institutionalization of YouTube: From User-Generated Content to Professionally Generated Content." *Media, Culture & Society* 34 (1): 53–67. doi:10.1177/0163443711427199.

Kincaid, Jason. 2010. "EdgeRank: The Secret Sauce That Makes Facebook's Newsfeed Tick." *TechCrunch*. April 22. Accessed May 4, 2016. http://techcrunch.com/2010/04/22/facebook-edgerank/.

Kobrin, Mike. 2007. "Jamming at the Speed of Light." *Wired*. January 31. http://archive.wired.com/software/coolapps/news/2007/01/72612.

Lampinen, Airi. 2015. "Deceptively Simple: Unpacking the Notion of 'Sharing.'" *Social Media + Society* 1 (1). doi:10.1177/2056305115578135.

Law, John. 2009. "Actor-Network Theory and Material Semiotics." In *The New Blackwell Companion to Social Theory*, edited by Bryan S. Turner, 141–58. Blackwell Companions to Sociology. Malden, MA: Wiley-Blackwell.

Leadbeater, Charles. 2009. *We-Think: [Mass Innovation, Not Mass Production]*. 2nd ed. London: Profile Books.

Lee, Micky. 2011. "Google Ads and the Blindspot Debate." *Media, Culture & Society* 33 (3): 433–47. doi:10.1177/0163443710394902.

Lenhart, Amanda, Mary Madden, Aaron Smith, Kristen Purcell, Kathryn Zickuhr, and Lee Rainie. 2011. "Teens, Kindness and Cruelty on Social Network Sites." Washington, DC: Pew Research Center. http://www.pewinternet.org/files/old-media//Files/Reports/2011/PIP_Teens_Kindness_Cruelty_SNS_Report_Nov_2011_FINAL_110711.pdf.

Leonard, Andrew. 2013. "How Netflix Is Turning Viewers into Puppets." *Salon*. February 1. http://www.salon.com/2013/02/01/how_netflix_is_turning_viewers_into_puppets/.

Levine, Elana. 2008. "Distinguishing Television: The Changing Meanings of Television Liveness." *Media, Culture & Society* 30 (3): 393–409. doi:10.1177/0163443708088794.

Lotz, Amanda. 2014. *The Television Will Be Revolutionized*. 2nd ed. New York: New York University Press.

Maclean, Andrew. 2013. "Your Startup Name Matters (A Lot) [VIDEO]." *Inc.com*. January 29. http://www.inc.com/max-haot.html.

Mangalindan, J. P. 2011. "Timeline: Where Facebook Got Its Funding." *Forbes*. January 11. http://fortune.com/2011/01/11/timeline-where-facebook-got-its-funding/.

Manovich, Lev. 2013. *Software Takes Command: [Extending the Language of New Media]*. International Texts in Critical Media Aesthetics 5. New York: Bloomsbury.

Marriott, Stephanie. 2007. *Live Television: Time, Space and the Broadcast Event*. Los Angeles: Sage.

Matsa, Katerina Eva, and Amy Mitchell. 2014. "8 Key Takeaways about Social Media and News." *Pew Research Center Journalism & Media*. March 26. http://www.journalism.org/2014/03/26/8-key-takeaways-about-social-media-and-news/.

McCarthy, Anna. 2001. *Ambient Television: Visual Culture and Public Space*. Durham, NC: Duke University Press.

McPherson, Tara. 2002. "Reload: Liveness, Mobility and the Web." In *The Visual Culture Reader*, 2nd ed., edited by Nicholas Mirzoeff, 458–72. New York: Routledge.

Meyrowitz, Joshua. 1986. *No Sense of Place: The Impact of Electronic Media on Social Behavior*. New York: Oxford University Press.

Miller, Liz Shannon. 2013. "How *Orange Is the New Black* Is Keeping the Buzz Alive." August 18. https://gigaom.com/2013/08/18/how-orange-is-the-new-black-is-keeping-the-buzz-alive/.

Mitchell, Amy, Tom Rosenstiel, and Leah Christian. 2012. "What Facebook and Twitter Mean for News." Washington, DC: State of the News Media. http://stateofthemedia.org/2012/mobile-devices-and-news-consumption-some-good-signs-for-journalism/what-facebook-and-twitter-mean-for-news/.

Morozov, Evgeny. 2011. *The Net Delusion: The Dark Side of Internet Freedom*. New York: Public Affairs.

Morse, Margaret. 1998. *Virtualities: Television, Media Art, and Cyberculture*. Bloomington: Indiana University Press.

Müller, Eggo. 2009. "Formatted Spaces of Participation: Interactive Television and the Changing Relationship between Production and Consumption." In *Digital Material: Tracing New Media in Everyday Life*, edited by Marianne van den Boomen, Sybille Lammes, Ann-Sophie Lehmann, Joost Raessens, and Mirko Tobias Schäfer, 49–63. Amsterdam: Amsterdam University Press.

Mumford, L. S. 1994. "Stripping on the Girl Channel: Lifetime, *Thirtysomething*, and Television Form." *Camera Obscura: Feminism, Culture, and Media Studies* 11-12 (3-1 33-34): 166–91. doi:10.1215/02705346-11-12-3-1_33-34-166.

Napoli, Philip M. 2011. *Audience Evolution: New Technologies and the Transformation of Media Audiences*. New York: Columbia University Press.

Nededog, Jethro. 2011. "'The Voice': 10 Things Said and Heard in the Pressroom." *Zap2it*. June 8. http://www.zap2it.com/blogs/the_voice_10_things_said_and_heard_in_the_pressroom-2011-06.

Needleman, Rafe. 2007. "eJamming: Skype for Musicians." *CNET*. January 30. http://www.cnet.com/news/ejamming-skype -for-musicians/.

Norman, Donald A. 1988. *The Design of Everyday Things*. New York: Doubleday.

O'Reilly, Tim. 2012. "What Is Web 2.0? Design Patterns and Business Models for the Next Generation of Software." In *The Social Media Reader*, edited by Michael Mandiberg, 32–52. New York: New York University Press.

Palmer, Daniel. 2003. "The Paradox of User Control." Talk presented at the International Digital Arts and Culture Conference, Melbourne, Australia, May 19.

Pariser, Eli. 2012. *The Filter Bubble: How the New Personalized Web Is Changing What We Read and How We Think*. New York: Penguin.

Parr, Ben. 2009. "Live Video Service Mogulus Reinvents Itself as Livestream.com." *Mashable*. May 19. http://mashable.com/2009/ 05/18/livestream-mogulus/.

———. 2013. "Zuckerberg's Vision Realized: One Graph to Rule Them All." *CNET*. January 16. http://www.cnet.com/news/ zuckerbergs-vision-realized-one-graph-to-rule-them-all/.

Pearson, Roberta. 2011. "Cult Television as Digital Television's Cutting Edge." In *Television as Digital Media*, edited by James Bennett and Niki Strange, 105–31. Durham, NC: Duke University Press.

Petersen, Søren Mørk. 2008. "Loser Generated Content: From Participation to Exploitation." *First Monday* 13 (4). http://www. firstmonday.dk/ojs/index.php/fm/article/view/2141/1948.

Puijk, Roel. 2010. "What Happened to Media Events." Talk presented at the NECS, Kadir Has University, Istanbul, Turkey, June 25.

Quintana, Melody. 2010. "Facebook Tips: What's the Difference between Top News and Most Recent?" *Facebook Blog*. August 6. http://blog.facebook.com/blog.php?post=414305122130.

Reckhow, Michael. 2015. "Introducing Instant Articles." *Facebook Blog*. May 12. http://media.fb.com/2015/05/12/instantarticles/.

Renaud, Alain, Alexander Carôt, and Pedro Rebelo. 2007. "Networked Music Performance: State of the Art." Talk presented at the AES 30th International Conference, Saariselka, Finland, March 15.

"A Report on Internet Speeds in All 50 States." 2010. Washington, DC: Communications Workers of America. http://cwa. bluestatedigital.com/page/-/SPEEDMATTERS/Publications /2010SpeedTestReportFullFINAL.pdf?nocdn=1.

Rieder, Bernhard, and Guillaume Sire. 2014. "Conflicts of Interest and Incentives to Bias: A Microeconomic Critique of Google's Tangled Position on the Web." *New Media & Society* 16 (2): 195–211. doi:10.1177/1461444813481195.

Rogers, Richard. 2013. *Digital Methods*. Cambridge, MA: MIT Press.

Rose, Frank. 2012. *The Art of Immersion: How the Digital Generation Is Remaking Hollywood, Madison Avenue, and the Way We Tell Stories*. New York: Norton.

Rushkoff, Douglas. 2011. *Program or Be Programmed: Ten Commands for a Digital Age*. Berkeley, CA: Soft Skull Press.

Salmon, Felix. 2011. "The Hermetic and Arrogant New York Times." *Reuters*, May 8. http://blogs.reuters.com/felix-salmon/2011/05/08/the-hermetic-and-arrogant-new-york-times/.

Sanghvi, Ruchi. 2006. "Facebook Gets a Facelift." *Facebook Blog*. September 5. https://blog.facebook.com/blog.php?post=2207967130.

Scannell, Paddy. 2001. "Authenticity and Experience." *Discourse Studies* 3 (4): 405–11. doi:10.1177/1461445601003004005.

———. 2014. *Television and the Meaning of Live: An Enquiry into the Human Situation*. Malden, MA: Polity.

Schäfer, Mirko Tobias. 2011. *Bastard Culture!: How User Participation Transforms Cultural Production*. MediaMatters. Amsterdam: Amsterdam University Press.

Schiffman, Betsy. 2007. "Status Update: Facebook Is Letting Users Drop the 'Is.'" *Wired*. November 20. http://www.wired.com/2007/11/status-update-f/.

Schmaus, Warren. 2004. *Rethinking Durkheim and His Tradition*. Cambridge: Cambridge University Press.

Scholz, Trebor. 2008. "Market Ideology and the Myths of Web 2.0." *First Monday* 13 (3). http://firstmonday.org/article/view/2138/1945.

Sengupta, Somini. 2012. "Facebook Reports a Loss, but Its Revenue Beats Expectations." *New York Times*, July 26. http://www.nytimes.com/2012/07/27/technology/facebook-reports-a-loss-but-its-revenue-beats-expectations.html.

Shirky, Clay. 2009. *Here Comes Everybody: The Power of Organizing without Organizations [with an Updated Epilogue]*. Nachdr. New York: Penguin.

Slutsky, Irina, and Kunur Patel. 2011. "Is Social Media Killing TV?" *AdAge*. April 18. http://adage.com/article/digital/social-media-killing-tv/227028/.

Smythe, Dallas W. 1977. "Communications: Blind Spot of Western Marxism." *Canadian Journal of Political and Social Theory* 3 (1): 1–28.

Steinberg, Brian. 2009a. "Socially Awkward TV Efforts Point to the Future." *AdAge*. September 14. http://adage.com/article/media/media-fox-twee-peat-found-bulky-points-future/138966/.

———. 2009b. "First Network, Then Cable, Now There's 'Social TV.'" *AdAge*. November 16. http://adage.com/article/media/network-cable-social-tv/140545/.

Stone, Brad. 2007. "Microsoft Buys Stake in Facebook." *New York Times*, October 25. http://www.nytimes.com/2007/10/25/technology/25facebook.html.

Taibi, Catherine. 2015. "Super Bowl XLIX Was Most-Watched Show in U.S. Television History." *Huffington Post*. February 2. http://social.huffingtonpost.com/2015/02/02/super-bowl-tv-ratings-2015-patriots-seahawks_n_6595690.html.

Tapscott, Don, and Anthony D. Williams. 2010. *Wikinomics: How Mass Collaboration Changes Everything*. Expanded ed. New York: Portfolio/Penguin.

Taylor, Chris. 2012. "Facebook Has 955 Million Active Users—Still Shy of a Billion." *Mashable*. July 26. http://mashable.com/2012/07/26/facebook-955-million-users/.

Terranova, Tiziana. 2004. *Network Culture: Politics for the Information Age*. Ann Arbor, MI: Pluto Press.

Thompson, John B. 1995. *The Media and Modernity: A Social Theory of the Media*. Cambridge: Polity Press in association with Blackwell Publishers.

Toffler, Alvin. 1990. *The Third Wave*. New York: Bantam Books.

Tonkelowitz, Mark. 2011. "Interesting News, Any Time You Visit." *Facebook Blog*. September 20. https://blog.facebook.com/blog.php?post=10150286921207131.

Trainer, David. 2016. "Twitter's Business Model Remains Broken, Stock Price Too High." *Forbes*. February 12. http://www.forbes.com/sites/greatspeculations/2016/02/12/twitters-business-model-remains-broken-stock-price-too-high/.

Turner, Graeme. 2009. "Television and the Nation: Does This Matter Any More?" In *Television Studies after TV: Understanding Television in the Post-Broadcast Era*, edited by Graeme Turner and Jinna Tay, 54–64. New York: Routledge.

Turner, Graeme, and Jinna Tay. 2009. "Introduction." In *Television Studies after TV: Understanding Television in the Post-Broadcast Era*, edited by Graeme Turner and Jinna Tay, 1–6. New York: Routledge.

Uricchio, William. 2004. "Television's Next Generation: Technology / Interface Culture / Flow." In *Television after TV: Essays on a Medium in Transition*, edited by Lynn Spigel and Jan Olsson, 232–61. Durham, NC: Duke University Press.

————. 2009. "Contextualizing the Broadcast Era: Nation, Commerce, and Constraint." *The Annals of the American Academy of Political and Social Science* 625 (1): 60–73. doi:10.1177/0002716209339145.

————. 2011. "The Algorithmic Turn: Photosynth, Augmented Reality and the Changing Implications of the Image." *Visual Studies* 26 (1): 25–35.

Van Buskirk, Eliot. 2007. "Finally, the On-Demand, Online Garage Band Gets Real." *Wired*. April 30. http://archive.wired.com/entertainment/music/commentary/listeningpost/2007/04/listeningpost_0430.

van den Boomen, Marianne. 2007. "What Is Web 2.0?" *Meta Blog-Note*. April 22. http://metamapping.net/blog/?p=85#more-85.

van Dijck, José. 2007. "Television 2.0: YouTube and the Emergence of Homecasting." Talk presented at the MIT 5, Cambridge, Massachusetts, April 27.

————. 2011. "Tracing Twitter: The Rise of a Microblogging Platform." *International Journal of Media & Cultural Politics* 7 (3): 333–48. doi:10.1386/macp.7.3.333_1.

————. 2013a. *The Culture of Connectivity: A Critical History of Social Media*. Oxford: Oxford University Press.

————. 2013b. "Facebook and the Engineering of Connectivity: A Multi-Layered Approach to Social Media Platforms." *Convergence: The International Journal of Research into New Media Technologies* 19 (2): 141–55. doi:10.1177/1354856512457548.

van Dijck, José, and David Nieborg. 2009. "Wikinomics and Its Discontents: A Critical Analysis of Web 2.0 Business Manifestos." *New Media & Society* 11 (5): 855–74. doi:10.1177/1461444809105356.

van Dijck, José, and Thomas Poell. 2013. "Understanding Social Media Logic." *Media and Communication* 1 (1): 2–14.

van Es, Karin. 2015. "The Promise and Perils of Social TV: The Participation Dilemma in NBC's *The Voice*." *Television and New Media*, first published on November 30 as doi: 10.1177/1527476415616191.

van Es, Karin, and Eggo Müller. 2012. "THE VOICE: Über das 'Soziale' des sozialen Fernsehens." *Montage/AV* 1 (20): 63–84.

Vianello, Robert. 1985. "The Power Politics of 'Live' Television." *Journal of Film and Television* 37 (3): 26–40.

"*Washington Post*-Pew Research Center Poll." n.d. *Washington Post*. http://www.washingtonpost.com/wp-srv/politics/polls/postpoll_05022011.html.

Weltevrede, Esther, Anne Helmond, and Carolin Gerlitz. 2014. "The Politics of Real-Time: A Device Perspective on Social Media

Platforms and Search Engines." *Theory, Culture & Society* 31 (6): 125–50. doi:10.1177/0263276414537318.

White, Michele. 2006. "Television and Internet Differences by Design: Rendering Liveness, Presence, and Lived Space." *Convergence: The International Journal of Research into New Media Technologies* 12 (3): 341–55. doi:10.1177/1354856506067206.

White, Mimi. 2004. "The Attractions of Television: Reconsidering Liveness." In *MediaSpace: Place, Scale and Culture in a Media Age*, edited by Nick Couldry and Anna McCarthy, 75–92. London: Routledge.

Willson, Michele. 2014. "The Politics of Social Filtering." *Convergence: The International Journal of Research into New Media Technologies* 20 (2): 218–32. doi:10.1177/1354856513479761.

Wu, Tim. 2013. "Netflix's War on Mass Culture." *New Republic*, December 4. http://www.newrepublic.com/article/115687/netflixs-war-mass-culture.

Ytreberg, Espen. 2009. "Extended Liveness and Eventfulness in Multi-Platform Reality Formats." *New Media & Society* 11 (4): 467–85. doi:10.1177/1461444809102955.

Yung, Raylene. 2009. "New Views for Your Home Page." *Facebook Blog*. October 23. https://blog.facebook.com/blog.php?post=162536657130.

Zettl, Herbert. 1978. "The Rare Case of Television Aesthetics." *Journal of the University Film Association* 30 (2): 3–8.

Zimmer, Michael. 2008. "The Externalities of Search 2.0: The Emerging Privacy Threats When The Drive For the Perfect Search Engine Meets Web 2.0." *First Monday* 13 (3). http://firstmonday.org/article/view/2136/1944.

Zittrain, Jonathan. 2008. *The Future of the Internet and How to Stop It*. New Haven, CT: Yale University Press.

Index

Note: Page numbers in **bold type** indicate figures

ABC (American Broadcasting
  Company) 9, 89
Academy Awards 86, 108
Adams, Frank (Livestream
  user) 51
Aguilera, Christina 91,
  170n(72)
Al Jazeera English, 169n(54)
Alang, Navneet 129–30
algorithm(s) 31–2, 119, 123,
  126, 135, 137–8, 143–4,
  146–8, 158, 159,
  172n(88)
  adaptive 132
  (de)compression 72
  selection through 17, 133
Alpha House (series) 118–19
Amazon 119, 143, 147
Amazon Prime 4
Amazon Studios 118, 119,
  157, 158
American Idol (series) 4
Andrejevic, Mark 24, 47, 131,
  146
ANT (actor-network theory)
  25, 26–7
Apple *see* iTunes

Arrested Development
  (series) 117
audience(s) 2, 3, 4, 5, 10, 11,
  13, 16, 28, 32, 38, 40,
  45, 52, 53, 54, 61, 62,
  63, 76, 78, 79, 80, 83,
  85, 86, 88, 89, 90, 93,
  94, 95, 96, 97, 98, 100,
  101, 102, 105, 106, 108,
  109, 110, 113, 117, 118,
  119, 121, 122, 128, 145,
  150, 153, 154,157,
  167n(29)
  conflict among 103, 105,
  107, 108
  fragmentation 62, 85, 86,
  87
  live 98, 101, 102, 110, 112
  participation 17, 84, 89, 95,
  99, 108, 114, 120–2,
  144, 156, 157, 158
Auslander, Philip 2, 5, 7, 8, 9,
  10, 11, 21, 71

bandwidth 44, 70, 126,
  166n(20)
  cost of 49

Bergman, Cory 106, 108, 170n(58)
Berners-Lee, Tim 164n(8)
Berry, David M. 164n(8)
Betas (series) 118–19
Big Bang Theory, The (series) 85, 169(n53)
Big Brother (series) 29
Bin Laden, Osama 140, 171–2nn(86–7)
BlogTV 37
Boddy, William 12
Bourdieu, Pierre 19, 21
Bourdon, Jérôme 3, 5, 156
boyd, danah 125, 126, 142–3
Boyle, Susan 145
Breaking Bad (series) 117, 171n(76)
Brightcove 55
Britain's Got Talent (series) 145
Broadcast Decency Enforcement Act (US 2005) 9
broadcast TV
  care structure of 11
  live programming in 4
  democratizing 16, 54
  emulating 36–50
  future of 122
  rhythms and temporalities of 115–19
  strategy of 84–7, 90
  see also event TV; television; social TV
Bruns, Axel 86, 89, 109
Bucher, Taina 31, 129, 132, 137, 165n(16), 171n(83)
Burgess, Jean 165n(9)

Caldwell, John T. 1, 3, 5, 13, 88, 156, 162
Callon, Michel 25
care structure(s) 11, 36
  hidden/invisible 154
Carlson, Nicholas 47, 48–9

Carôt, Alexander 71
Cartman (eJamming user) 80
CBS (Columbia Broadcasting System) 8–9, 89, 163n(2)
Charlier, Philippe 25
check-in apps 90
cinema(s) 1, 11, 155
Classmates.com 124
Colon, Javier 109–10
copyright 33, 47, 74
  infringement 48
  violation 50
Couldry, Nick 4–5, 7, 13, 15, 18–21, 27, 36, 44, 145, 150, 159, 160
creator tools 37, 44–6
cross-media 90
cultural forces 30, 151
  see also sociocultural forces; techno-cultural forces

Daly, Carson 91–5, 99, 103, 104, 120, 121
data-driven decision-making 17, 119, 157
deep media 90
Deleuze, Gilles 25
Digital Millennium Copyright Act (US 1998) 47
dispositif(s) 25, 26
Dixon, Steve 9
DMCA *see* Digital Millennium Copyright Act
dotcom-bubble bust 22
Driessen, Peter F. 70, 168n(40)
Durkheim, Emile 27, 165n(12)
DVR (digital video recorder) 4, 59, 106, 115

economic force(s) 29, 32–3, 44, 46, 69, 153, 155
EdgeRank 126, 137–8
Egaas, Aaron (*The Voice* viewer) 108

Eitzen, Dirk 164n(5)
eJamming 9, 14, 16, 32,
    64–82, 108, 152, 153,
    167nn(34/38),
    168nn(43–7), 173
    AUDiiO 65, 67, 72, 77
    home page snapshot 66
    metatext of 65–9
    space of participation of
        69–75
    user responses to 75–82
Ellis, John 7, 13
Emmy Awards 108
Enli, Gunn Sara 171n(78)
enveloping 87, 89–90, 91, 94,
    95, 100, 101, 108
EPT (ensemble performance
    threshold) 70, 71
Erickson, Christine 118, 139
EULAs (End-User License
    Agreements) 33
ER (series) 3
event TV 4, 62, 97, 122
exposure metrics 122
extension(s) 87–8, 89, 93, 95,
    99, 101

Facebook 14, 22, 53, 57, 59,
    92, 96, 99, 151, 152,
    158, 169n(57),
    171n(80), 172n(89),
    174
    algorithms of 135, 143, 147,
        159
    metatext of 124–26
    monetization of 129, 141
    penetration of 171n(84)
    privacy policies/issues with
        131–2, 139–42, 143
    real-name policy 131
    space of participation of
        126–38
    user responses to 139–42
    see also Facebook features;
        Zuckerberg

Facebook Blog 124, 132, 133,
    134, 135, 136
Facebook features
    Chat 127, 128, 153
    Facebook Blog 124, 132,
        133, **134**, 135
    Most Recent 133, 134–5,
        136, 138, 148
    Open Graph 136, 138, 150
    Ticker 127, 133, 135–6,
        138, 142
    Timeline 124, 127, 132,
        138, 171n(85)
    Top News 134–5, 138, 148
    see also Live Feed; News
        Feed
FCC (US Federal
    Communications
    Commission) 9, 104,
    163n(1)
Fender 78, 167n(38)
Fenton, Natalie 63
Feuer, Jane 7, 12, 13
Filter bubble 147
Ford, Sam 144–5
Foucault, Michel 25
Fox television 4, 88, 117, 148
Fox news 148
Fringe (series) 88
Friedman, James 3
Fuchs, Christian 24, 131,
    165n(10)

Galloway, Alexander R. 24
Gannett Company 41
Gehl, Robert W. 124, 126
Genette, Gérard 28
geo-filtering 99
Gerlitz, Carolin, 123, 149,
    150
Gibson, James 30
Gillan, Jennifer 62, 87, 88,
    122
Gillespie, Tarleton 123, 159
Glee (series) 88

Glueckman, Alan 77,
    168n(43), 169n(48)
Golden Globes 108
Google 75, 147, 149
Google AdSense 32, 172n(89)
Google Analytics 60, 172n(89)
Grammy Awards 163n(2)
GraphRank 137, 138
Gray, Jonathan 28, 122,
    165n(13)
Green, Cee Lo 91, 109
Green, Joshua 144–5, 165n(9)
Grint, Keith 31
Grossman, Lev 126, 129

Haenlein, Michael 22
Haislip, Alison 91, 92, 94,
    95–7, 109, 120
Halavais, Alexander 147
Hallinan, Blake 118, 119
Halperin, Shirley 97, 106
Haot, Max 37, 38, 40, 49, 52,
    54, 55–6, 166n(23),
    167n(29), 173
Harrington, Stephen 86, 89
Heath, Stephen 6–7
Helmond, Anne 123, 149, 150
Highfield, Tim 86, 89
Hills, Matt 116–17, 118,
    164n(9)
Holder, Mitchell (*The Voice*
    viewer) 110
Hollywood Reporter, The 112
House of Cards (series) 117,
    118, 119
Hulu 4, 49
Hutchby, Ian 30–1
hypermediacy 88

indecency 9, 47, 48, 104,
    163n(1)
Instagram 33, 73, 125, 146
integration 41, 58, 87, 90–1,
    95, 100, 101, 120, 129,
    158, 164n(4)

internet 4, 12, 13, 18, 20, 22,
    24, 39, 44, 65, 69, 72,
    74, 76, 80, 86, 141
broadcasts over 73, 80
early statements
    about 167n(35)
inherent latency of the 71
Internet Archive *see* Wayback
    Machine
iTunes 94, 99, 111, 113,
    171n(75)

JackTrip 64
JamCastLive/JamCastle 73
Jenkins, Henry 23, 24–5, 33,
    87, 90, 115, 118,
    144–5, 164–5n(9)
JohnnySixString (eJamming
    user) 77, 78
just-in-time fandom 116–17,
    118
Justin.tv 37, 43

Kantor, Gail 77
Kaplan, Andreas M. 22
Kennedy, Jenny 125
Kincaid, Jason 137, 138
Knight, Erin (*The Voice*
    viewer) 105–6

latency 69, 70–3, 76–8, 80,
    82, 153, 168n(40)
Latour, Bruno 25
Law, John 25, 26
legal forces 33–4, 44, 69, 74,
    100, 130, 153
Leonard, Andrew 119
Levine, Adam 91, 93–4,
    103–4, 109, 110, 111
Levine, Elana 3–4, 12–13,
    114
Lilyhammer (series) 117
Linden Lab (3D Virtual World)
    67–8
LinkedIn 125

Live Feed (Facebook) 17, 112, 124, 132–3, 135, **134**, 137, 138
live music 66, 113
live performance 8, 110–11
live-streaming platforms 2, 50
    appeal of 155
    challenges facing 47–50
    YouTube and 47–9
    see also Livestream
liveness/the 'live'
    constellations of 18–34, 60
    domains of 27–8
    as evaluative category 64–82
    future of 160–2
    institutionalization of 15, 16, 35–63, 84, 128, 154
    media studies and 5–14
    paradox of 15, 16, 36, 113, 121, 154, 156
    social media's new relation to 123–51
    tension(s) surrounding 14, 16, 17, 81, 108, 115–22, 123, 156–60
    what, when, and how of 153–6
Livestream 53, 58, 64, 70, 152, 166n(27), 167nn(31–2), 173
    copyright issues with 74 *see also* Mogulus; New Livestream
Livestream Studio 45, 46
Livestream Support 51
Lotz, Amanda 4, 62, 84–5, 122

Manovich, Lev 159
Marriott, Stephanie 7, 9, 162
McPherson, Tara 5, 13
media power 15, 19–22, 25, 27
media studies 144, 159
    liveness as a concept in 5–14

metatext 15, 26, 28–9, 33, 34, 84, 110, 152
    of eJamming 65–9, 73, 75–7, 80–2, 153
    of Facebook 124–33, 139, 141
    of Mogulus/Original Livestream 36–50
    of New Livestream 54–7
    of *The Voice* 91–104, 107, 108
Meyrowitz, Joshua 7
MIDI (Musical Instrument Digital Interface) 69, 73
Milian, Christina 120
Mogulus/Original Livestream 15–16, 36–50, 57, 60–3, 74, 120, 128, 154, 166nn(17–18), 166n(20), 172n(88)
    home page snapshot 38
    metatext of 36–42
    space of participation of 42–50
    user responses to 50–54
    see also Haot; Procaster
Mogulus Studio 39, 45
monetization 4, 23, 41, 141
    challenges of 46–50
    strategies for 129
Morozov, Evgeny 24
Müller, Eggo 23, 26, 29–32, 165nn(9/14), 169n(51)
multiplatform formats 13
myth
    of the mediated center 20
    of "us" 20, 159, 160
    see also Couldry; media power; symbolic power

Napoli, Philip 122
NBC (National Broadcasting Company) 3, 4, 83, 89, 91, 103, 169nn(50/57)
    see also Voice, The

Netflix 4, 31, 117–19, 143, 157, 158
New Livestream 16, 49, 54–6, 57, 58, 59, 60, 61–3, 74, 154
  metatext of 54–6
  space of participation of 56–60
News Feed (Facebook) 123–7, 128, 132, **134**, 135, 136, 139, 144, 146, 148
  algorithms of 126, 137–8
  see also Live Feed
Nieborg, David 24
Nielsen Company 122, 169n(53)
NINJAM (Novel Intervallic Network Jamming Architecture for Music) 64, 71
Norman, Donald 30, 31

on-demand platforms 46
  live-streaming and 38, 43–4, 49, 51
  see also Netflix; VOD; YouTube
ontology 5, 12, 13, 25
  liveness as 6–9
Ooyala 55
Orange Is the New Black (series) 118
O'Reilly, Tim 22, 164n(8)
overlay(s) 37, 46, 49, 53, 87, 88–9, 90, 91, 93, 94, 95, 120

Palmer, Daniel 24, 131
paratext(s) 28–9, 165n(13)
Pariser, Eli 132, 147
Parr, Ben 41, 150
participation 4, 13, 91–101
  explicit 151
  implicit 130, 150–1
  see also audience participation; space of

participation; user participation
Peeters, Hugues 25
Petersen, Søren Mørk 24, 131
Pew Research Center 106, 139, 140–1
phenomenology 5, 25, 36
  liveness as 9–11,
Pinterest 73
Poell, Thomas 119, 147
privacy
  issues 139–42, 143, 144, 170n(61)
  policies 131–2
Procaster 45–6, 166n(21)

RaDiiO project 80
  see also eJamming
radio 2, 3, 7, 11, 12, 41, 55, 113
real time 9, 11, 16, 58, 60, 70, 71, 75, 76–77, 80, 85, 86, 89, 97, 102, 105, 108, 109, 119, 122, 136, 142
  liveness and 8, 16, 65, 82, 153
  social(ity) and 65, 68, 69, 76, 81, 114, 128, 155, 161
real-time web 123
Rebelo, Pedro 71
Reckhow, Michael 141
Renaud, Alain 70, 71
rhetoric 5, 19, 25, 39, 62, 93, 94, 110, 141, 159
  liveness as 11–14
Rieder, Bernhard 147–8
Rogers, Richard 159
Royal Opera House (Covent Garden) 1, 155

Salmon, Felix 171–2n(86)
Sanghvi, Ruchi 132, 137
Scannell, Paddy 1, 9, 11, 35–6, 54, 62, 112, 153–5

Schäfer, Mirko Tobias 24, 25–6, 31, 130, 150–1, 164n(7), 165n(9)
Schmaus, Warren 27, 155
Scholz, Trebor 24, 124, 131, 164n(8)
Second Life experiment 68, 80
Senna, Matthew (*The Voice* viewer) 107
series dumping 17, 117–18, 157
Shark Week (series) 89
Shelton, Blake 91, 93–4, 103, 109
Shirky, Clay 101
simulcasts 1, 2, 4, 11, 155
Sire, Guillaume 147–8
Skirrow, Gillian 6–7
Smythe, Dallas 32
social media
  broadcast media and 156–60
  relations between television and 87–91
    see also enveloping; extension(s); integration; overlay(s)
  user participation in the era of 22–5
    see also Facebook; Instagram; LinkedIn; Pinterest; Tumblr; Twitter; YouTube
social TV 4, 14, 16, 81
  and multiplicity of the live 83–122
  narrative of 85–7
  see also Voice, The
sociality 78–82, 153
  real time and 65, 69, 76, 81, 114, 128, 155, 161
space of participation 15, 25, 26, 28–33, 37, 84, 152, 165n(15), 166nn(19/24)
  for eJamming 66, 69–75, 81, 82
  for Facebook 126–32

for Mogulus/Original Livestream 42–50
for New Livestream 54
for Twitter 170n(60)
for *Voice, The* 91, 97–101, 107, 113, 114
for Volvo Ocean Race 56–61
spoilers 98, 107, 108, 116, 157
  and tape delay 103, 108
Sprint Skybox 120, **121**
Steinberg, Brian 86, 88
Stieglitz, Stefan 109
Striphas, Ted 118, 119
Super Bowl XLIX (2015) 86
Symbolic power 18–22, 115, 153, 159–60, 161

Talpa Productions 169n(50)
tape delay 84, 98, 103, 157, 163n(2)
  see also spoilers
Tapscott, Don 23
TechCrunch 54, 55–6, 137
techno-cultural forces 30–2, 44, 60, 69, 73, 144, 153
technological forces 29, 31, 82, 155
television 41, 52, 55
  live 1–2, 12, 35, 39, 101–11, 116, 157, 169n(55)
  phases in the history of 84–5
  social media and 87–91
  see also broadcast TV; event TV; social TV
Terranova, Tiziana 24, 131
The Voice see under Voice
Thompson, John B. 19, 21, 61, 164n(6)
Tilsner, Jamison 37
Tilzy.TV 37
Time 126, 129

time zones 98, 161, 169n(48),
170n(59), 174
multiple 84, 108, 157
Toffler, Alvin 23
transmedia storytelling 87, 90,
92
Trendistic (Twitter analysis
tool) 107
Tumblr 57
tweet-peat experiment 88
Twitter 2, 17, 43, 57, 86, 88,
89, 92, 95–9, 102, 103,
118, 123, 125, 144,
155, 160, 169n(57),
170nn(62–3/69–72),
174–5
activity around *The Voice* on
94, 100, 101, 107, 109,
112, 146
business model 129
live television and 103, 107–
10, 116, 157, 169n(55)
news 140–41
Twitter TV Ratings 122

Uricchio, William 84, 143–4,
169n(52)
user participation 19, 22–5,
69, 98, 123
user responses 15, 26, 28,
33–4, 37, 65, 66, 69,
115, 153
to eJamming 75–82
to Facebook 139–42
to Mogulus/Original
Livestream 50–4
to *The Voice* 101–12
Ustream.tv 37, 42, 43

Van Dijck, José 24, 26, 27, 31,
33, 53, 119, 124, 129,
139, 147, 164n(8),
165n(15), 170n(60)
Van Es, Karin 169n(51),
171n(77)

Varner, Jared (*The Voice*
viewer) 105
VCR (videocassette recorder)
3, 85, 115
see also DVR
Vianello, Robert 2, 3, 13
viewser(s) 83, 89, 92, 96, 97,
102, 109, 115, 157
VOD (video-on-demand) 4,
38, 48, 51, 115, 117
Voice, The 4, 14, 17, 32, 90,
105, **121**, 122,
169n(51), 170n(64),
171n(74), 174
metatext for 91–7
space of participation for
98–101
Twitter activity around 107,
109, 112, 146
different constructions of
liveness in the live
shows of 101–12, 113
user responses to 101–12
see also Aguilera; Daly;
Green; Haislip; Levine;
Milian; Shelton;
V-Room
Volvo Ocean Race *see* New
Livestream
V-Room (*The Voice*) 95–7,
120, 170n(62)
snapshot of **96**

Washington Post 140
Wayback Machine (Internet
Archive) 37, **38**, 55, **66**
Web 2.0 22–3, 164n(8)
Webcaster 45, 46, 166n(21)
Welch, Alice (*The Voice*
viewer) 110
White, Michele 5, 12
White, Mimi 7, 8, 13
Williams, Anthony D. 23
Willson, Michele 146, 148–9
Woolgar, Steve 31

World Cup 157
Wu, Tim 157, 167(n35)

YouTube 29, 32, 45, 68, 78–9,
    143, 145, 146, 173, 174
  live-streaming and 47–9
  see also YouTube Live
  Mogulus and 39, 40, 42, 43,
    166n(17)
  monitoring of user content
    on 48

YouTube Live 44
Ytreberg, Espen 5, 13, 86, 87,
    122

Zettl, Herbert 6
Zielinski, Becca (*The Voice*
    viewer) 103
Zittrain, Jonathan 24
Zuckerberg, Mark 124,
    126, 129, 142,
    150